WALKING
WITH THE
WISE

Real Estate

Investor

**27 Successful Mentors and Millionaires
Teach the Secrets of Real Estate Investing**

Compiled by

Linda Forsythe

MENTORS Publishing House, Inc.

Need Inspiration Information or Mentoring?

Visit our Web site!
www.mentorsmagazine.com

- **FREE** newsletters filled with guidance, from our nationally recognized mentors

- **FREE** online subscription to MENTORS magazine

- **FREE LIVE TELESEMINARS** by mentors and millionaires who interact and coach you toward success

- Connections with Mentors Worldwide

www.mentorsmagazine.com

Dedication

$\mathcal{W}$alking with the Wise Real Estate
Investor is dedicated
to anyone who has the desire
to be successful in Real Estate Investment
and to experience a life
of abundance.

WALKING WITH THE WISE *Real Estate Investor*

ISBN 0-9729875-3-3

Printed in the United States of America

7 6 5 4 3 2 1 – 1 0 9 8

Published by MENTORS Publishing House, Inc.

This book is available at quantity discounts for bulk purchases and for branding by businesses and organizations. For further information, or to learn more about Mentors magazine™, mentorsmagazine.com™, Walking with the Wise™ and other products and services of Mentors Publishing House, Inc, contact:

MENTORS Publishing House, Inc.
11115 Affinity Court, Suite 6
San Diego, CA 92131
Telephone: (858) 549-9222
e-mail: publications@mentorsmagazine.com
Web: www.mentorsmagazine.com

Graphic Design, Art Direction by Paul Taylor, Desktop Publishing Center
Mentors Lighthouse Logo Design by Sam Defais
Illustrations by Kim Muslusky

The publisher would like to acknowledge the many publishers and individuals who granted us permission to reprint their cited material or have written specifically for this book.

Foreword

Real Estate
Meets Reality

by Todd Dotson

When Linda Forsythe of Mentor's Magazine asked me to write the Foreword to *Walking With the Wise Real Estate Investor*, along with an accompanying article on real estate mentoring, my response was an immediate "Yes!" I consider it a great honor and truly a privilege.

While the number of books on real estate investing continues to grow each day, this is not just another book destined to clutter the shelves. *Walking With the Wise Real Estate Investor* is a rare assembly of the country's top real estate investors and trainers from innovative dealmaker Donald Trump to pioneering real estate trainer Ron LeGrand.

Real estate investing is constantly evolving, so today's investor must continue to seek education with training that transcends generic books, tapes, and weekend boot camps. It has long been my opinion that reality-based training is the only area of real estate education that investors should consider. Everything else just causes confusion, doubt, and ultimately failure. Investors need a surefire system coupled with a strategic plan for implementation that actually works in the trenches, not just when it is being sold from the stage.

Trust me when I tell you that I understand a thing or two about reality-based training and what it takes to succeed in the trenches where it matters most. As the developer of the nation's first on-site real estate mentoring program, I have had the unique opportunity of having worked in every major market in the country. I wasn't there simply selling books and tapes as many trainers have done. I was actually on the ground helping my students create immediate cash and assisting them in building sustainable wealth. Each week I send the mentors on my team to cities across the country to help both beginning and seasoned investors alike: Get In, Get Out, and Get Paid! In addition, each month I train hundreds of students at my boot camps teaching the fundamentals of reality-based real estate investing. I'm not talking about a lot of "show" — just the "go." Before I forget, be sure to read my article on Tactical Mentoring — What if the Navy SEALS taught Real Estate?

5

These experiences together with my operational experience in markets across the country enable me to quickly determine what is truly reality-based. I'm pleased to report that I have worked with a number of the contributing authors of *Walking With the Wise Real Estate Investor* who are actually doers and have a reality-based platform. I know because I've had the privilege to provide personal mentoring to many of their students, and I find that their students always come eager and well prepared.

All experts in their own right, each of the authors is covering a particular topic or area of specialty. You'll find a number of similarities and some differences between the authors in both their methodology and material. Be sure to read through the entire book and find an area of interest or an author that resonates with you.

Whether you are starting out, starting over, or striving to stay on top, remaining on the cutting edge with ongoing reality-based education is the key to lasting success. How can you tell if the training you have been exposed to passes the test?

Reality-based training is almost always comprised of five essential ingredients:
1) Field-tested in today's real estate market;
2) Updated constantly with real-time feedback;
3) Audited results that are measurable and easily verifiable;
4) Implemented quickly regardless of the market; and
5) Duplicated consistently by the average investor.

Working with an experienced investor and trainer who is reality-based will not only help you collapse the timeframes associated with your next deal, but it will ultimately fast track and ensure your success.

Keep in mind that no system, regardless of how reality-based, will provide the results you want without action on your part. If it were easy, then everybody would be a real estate millionaire. It's not easy, but I promise you it is worthwhile. Many of you may not want to hear that it is going to take some work on your part. If that's you, then I suggest you get over it or move on to something else.

Many of the contributing authors of *Walking With the Wise Real Estate Investor* offer additional books, tapes, and training that will enhance your success. I can be contacted at 1-800-RE-DEALS or www.TacticalRealEstate.com. So commit to continuing your education, working hard, staying focused, and maintaining your enthusiasm. If you do, someday you may be writing a Foreword and chapter in a book just like this one!

Acknowledgements
And Many Thanks...

Stephen Roulac — Welcome to Mentors International as our new business partner for global licensing! Thank you for contributing your genius in the legal, financial, strategic and organizational systems planning. We are now a worldwide conglomerate!

Ron LeGrand — You are the reason this book was created! Thank you for your guidance on who would be appropriate candidates for article contributors. Your rags to riches story and practical investment knowledge has inspired many to live "the good life."

Todd Dotson — For developing a phenomenal mentoring program for Real Estate Investors. Your one-on-one approach to teaching this type of investing takes the fear out of the unknown! Thank you for taking the time to personally mentor me on this fascinating income stream.

Cheri Hoffman — For being the Editor-In-Chief of the century!!! Thank you for working with every article contributor, (a huge task in itself). Thank you for making sure that what was written by each contributor was worthy to be printed in a book with high standards. It takes talent and patience to edit well known professionals!

Judy Hoffman — For being Cheri's mom and my good friend. Thank you for taking over for Cheri while on vacation and keeping this project moving foreward!

Paul Taylor — For being an incredible art director and graphic designer. It is because of you that our magazines and books are completed in record time and the finished products have a great look.

Mentors Magazine Webmasters — For making MENTORS magazine *THE* leader in the industry by creating, engineering and maintaining MENTORS on the Internet. (www.mentorsmagazine.com) All of you have worked together as a "well oiled machine" to create our multi-million dollar site and bringing mentoring information to the world.

Tiffany Young — For being my executive assistant and the Mentors teleseminar program director. Thank you for keeping everything in line by running smoothly. Your organizational and public relation skills are phenomenal! You are an asset to all of us at Mentors International.

Dan Kennedy — For taking the time from your very busy schedule to support and guide me. You've taught me so much and are a constant source of inspiration. I will always cherish our friendship.

Our article contributors — For taking the time from your very busy schedules to provide words of wisdom that will change the lives of all who read them. You are all angels!

With Love and Gratitude,

Linda Forsythe

TABLE OF CONTENTS

FOREWORD

ACKNOWLEDGEMENTS

SECTION I — CASTLES, DREAMS, AND YOUR FUTURE

"Successful Mentors guide you toward abundance using Real Estate Investment."

SECTION II — SURPRISE BONUS SECTION

Ron LeGrand Cover Story:
World's Leading Expert on Quick-Turn Real Estate
interviewed by Linda Forsythe 142

$\mathcal{W}$hoever walks with the wise...
will become wise
Whoever walks with fools...
will suffer harm.

Proverbs 13:20

But Wisdom is shown to be truth
by what results from it.

Matthew 11:19

Castles, Dreams, and Your Future

*"Successful Mentors guide you toward abundance
using Real Estate Investment"*

Renegade Millionaires

by Dan Kennedy

Over the past two years, in preparation for recording a new series of audio tapes, I've been reviewing notes from my 29 years of consulting work. I've focused on the more than 100 first generation "from scratch" millionaire and multi-millionaire entrepreneurs with whom I've worked closely. I have been able to identify commonalities among them.

I call them "Renegade Millionaires" because, in various ways, they deliberately defy their own industry norms as well as defying the prerequisites most people, including those in academia, believe necessary for creating success and wealth. Very few have any educational, apprenticeship or other background for the businesses they launch and prosper in; most are self-taught. For example, Ron LeGrand, a long-time client of mine and written about elsewhere in this book, made his fortune in real estate. His qualifications and background? None. He was a car mechanic.

This parallels my own experience. I have achieved notable success in four career fields — speaking, consulting, direct-response copywriting and publishing. No MBA; just a high school education. I could fill the entire chapter with other, similar examples of people without relevant backgrounds and with few resources — only resourcefulness — who have quickly created wealth. Further, as I said, they typically defy industry norms and general business norms. A number of them, for example, mimic my now-legendary "intentional inaccessibility," rather than being readily accessible.

If you line up the more than 100 Renegade Millionaires in a circle at one time, in one place, and inspect them, interview them, or eavesdrop on their conversations with each other, you will be first struck by their differences and diversity, not their commonalities. To the untrained, casual observer, there's nothing useful to learn because they are so different from each other. Admittedly, their commonalities are relatively few, but instructive.

First, about the differences. Some live like "the millionaire next door" profiled in Thomas Stanley's book of that title. They live modestly. By observation only, you might not guess them wealthy. Others live very flamboyantly, their wealth visibly displayed in luxury homes, luxury cars, private jets, lavish parties. It's a contrast like the one between the late Sam Walton, founder of Wal-Mart, and Donald Trump. Some have very large companies, with dozens to hundreds of employees, generating ten to hundreds of millions of dollars in yearly revenues. Others are more like me, with only one or two or even no employees, relatively low gross revenues but very high net margins, and seven figure annual personal incomes. Some live in major cities, others in towns so small there's no hotel and just one stop light. Some are as young as 30, others as old as 70. Married, single. In high tech, in very low tech. A few with advanced degrees, some college educated, most high school only, a few high school drop-outs. These differences are not useful, not instructive, other than to demonstrate that there is no particular resume requirement to join the club.

Now, about the commonalities. Most are not found in background, resume, or even choice of type of business activity or lifestyle. The commonalities are hidden, because they are largely attitudinal and behavioral. It is my contention that behaviors matter most. They are what can be identified and emulated. That is the subject of my Renegade Millionaire System, which you can obtain information about at www.renegademillionaire.com. For this book's chapter, however, I'd like to point out several specific commonalities about money.

What Renegade Millionaires Do Differently with Money

Most business owners have their wealth captive in their own businesses. Renegade Millionaires operate quite differently. They extract wealth from the business to invest elsewhere. Space here does not permit explaining why this is so important, but I assure you, it is. In my Renegade Millionaire System, I teach the five money responsibilities of the entrepreneur, two of which are "LIBERATE cash" and "INVEST cash."

With that said, what do they do with the money? Well, here's a commonality directly relevant to this book: more than 80% are invested in real estate. And I confess, I was a Johnny-come-lately to doing so, to my detriment. Further, if you want to move up the wealth pyramid, get copies of the last two or three years of the annual "Wealthiest Americans" issues of Forbes Magazine, and carefully review the descriptions of the 100 wealthiest individuals. You'll probably be surprised by the diversity, by the many who did not inherit. You should note how many list real estate investments.

People like my clients Ron LeGrand, Jeff Kaller, Ted Thomas, Chuck Smith, and Darin Garman, have created and are constantly creating legions of new, "from scratch" millionaires whose sole entrepreneurial expertise is real estate investing. They have had such massive marketplace impact, it's hard to find a city or town without their "We Buy Houses For Cash" signage and advertising. They have had such massive marketplace impact, they are a much-discussed thorn in the side of the licensed professional realtors who only help others buy and sell real estate for commission.

13

But outside of that, a commonality among most of the multi-millionaires who began creating their wealth through diverse other businesses is that they are "on-the-side" active real estate entrepreneurs, or at the very least, passive real estate investors.

The active/passive issue is a discussion subject unto itself because another "secret" money commonality among Renegade Millionaires is that they strive to turn the same dollar over as many times as possible. Ordinary entrepreneurs let a lot of dollars sit idle, inside their businesses, and in outside investments. Renegade Millionaires hate lazy money. Our premise is that our money should work much harder for us than we worked to obtain it in the first place. So, many follow Ron LeGrand's premise: don't buy to hold, buy to sell.

Consider four different dollars. One stays captive in a business until the business is sold. Over 20 years, if the business increases 100 times in value, the dollar becomes one hundred dollars. However, during that entire 20-year term, its owner has not had any use of the dollar whatsoever.

Another dollar comes out of the business into a relatively conservative, interest-bearing device, earning 5% a year and compounding. Over 20 years, it will be worth substantially more than the dollar left in the business — but still, it will take 20 years.

A third dollar goes into real estate that appreciates by 5% a year or more, but also kicks out current income. That's the hardest working, most valuable of the three dollars. But the fourth dollar goes into real estate that is "flipped" in 30 days at a 30% profit, thus becoming $1.33. Then a month later it is turned into $1.72, and a month later $2.23 … you do the rest of the math, month by month, for just a few years. For ten years. Further, only the third and fourth dollars can be leveraged; the dollar "down" controlling perhaps five or ten dollars worth of real estate. This begins to explain why liberating money from business is important, and why so many Renegade Millionaires are attracted to active real estate entrepreneurship, not just passive real estate investment.

This is just one of many examples of ways Renegade Millionaires think differently about money.

Let me quickly explore three more.

No Such Thing as a "Bad Economy"

Quite a few of my clients launched businesses and got rich during the Carter Administration recession, with double digit inflation, sky high interest rates, dried up capital. We recognize that there are different economies, an always changing economy, and that good news in one place is always paralleled by bad news in another. None of that matters much to us. Bluntly, winners win and losers lose and whiners whine and excuse makers make excuses. They do what they do. We do what we do. What we have in common is doing it regardless of the economic conditions occurring at the moment.

Appreciate the Infinite, Abundant Supply of Wealth

Wealth is flowing through the economy, swirling around us. Most people insist on viewing money as a finite, limited resource that is hard to get, thus the horrid phrase "hard-earned money." Worse, most think of money as win/lose, a dollar gained as someone else's dollar lost; if the rich get richer, the poor must get poorer. Contrary to liberal and media nonsense, historical and current facts tell a very different story. And we Renegade Millionaires understand there's no limit. As my friend and "money teacher," the late Foster Hibbard used to say, "The vast ocean cares little whether you dip into it with spoon or bucket." Renegade Millionaires don't just think in terms of infinite abundance — they act on the belief. Any fool can lecture or write or posture about prosperity thinking, and many do. Few behave based on the premise of unlimited wealth there for the taking.

Invest Aggressively in Acquiring Customers

Whatever core business Renegade Millionaires are in, they invest aggressively in acquiring customers. There is a secret we know that 95% of all business owners do not. I can tell it to you here, but I lack space and time to sell it to you here, and it is so contrary to everything you've ever been taught and everything you believe you know about business, it requires lengthy explanation and persuasion. Suffice it to say that there is a profound difference between replaceable and irreplaceable assets, and most entrepreneurs err by over-investing in the first, under-investing in the second.

100-Million Dollars' Street Smarts, Channeled

I've been very fortunate, in my consulting business, to work up close, hands on, for extended periods — as long as 20 years — with over 100 different individuals who started businesses from scratch and created wealth. In my Renegade Millionaire System I answer the questions put to me in nearly 17 hours of interview, and I feel I am "channeling" all one hundred. In essence, I am channeling well over 100 million dollars' worth of street smart, experience-based strategy.

I've worked with people who have built businesses from zero to as much as $800 million a year in sales. With lots of "solo entrepreneurs" earning over a million dollars a year each, personally. With people who've gone from zero or even upside down to making over $100,000 a month in as short a time as 90 days. Here's one of the things I've seen repeated, over and over and over again.

The Sudden Income Explosion

Life's a marathon, but often wealth is a sprint. Sometimes it is a single scrap of new information. Sometimes a new stimulus of one kind of another. A book like this read, a seminar attended, a person met. One last puzzle piece dropping into place. Suddenly a person who may have had years of undistinguished results "blasts off" and achieves more in 90 days than in the previous 9 months, more in one year than in the previous ten years.

This is why Renegade Millionaires are obsessed with the acquisition of information. They know that something as "small" as one sentence might yield a huge business breakthrough or dramatic income explosion. This has occurred on five different occasions for me. In one case, an offhand remark made by a speaker, a remark he did not intend as teaching, caught by me, has been worth several million dollars to me. You could write what he said in fewer than 20 words on a 3 x 5″ card. I'm pleased to say that I've heard from hundreds of people that I have had that same affect on them — I know of instances where one sentence I've uttered in a coaching session has yielded hundreds of thousands of dollars, even transformed entire businesses. I've included many of these in my Renegade Millionaire System. Each consumes no more than one piece of paper. Each is enunciated in only a few words.

Anyway, here's the point: people DO "get rich quick." And you can too! You can suddenly sprint to wealth. You need the right information. Every circumstance is changed by information. Maybe you'll find your missing piece right here in this book. If by chance you found it in this chapter, let me know.

Dan S. Kennedy is a highly-paid direct-response copywriter, consultant, coach and advisor to thousands of his "Inner Circle Members" worldwide, and a confidante to over 100 first-generation, "from-scratch" millionaires and multi-millionaire entrepreneurs. He is the author of nine books, including the No B.S. *series of books published by Entrepreneur Press. Information about Dan is available at www.dankennedy.com.*

16

Private Lending

The Key to Freedom and Real Profit in Real Estate Investing

by Alan Cowgill

Within thirty days, you too could have a limitless supply of cash-on-hand to buy homes, regardless of your credit.

Most people don't realize it, but obtaining money for real estate deals has nothing to do with saving money for a down payment, going to a bank, filling out an application, and waiting to be approved. In fact, if you're going about things this way, as I did for many years, you're wasting time and losing money.

For me, discovering how to use private lenders in my real estate business has been truly life altering. The amount of money I make and the kind of work I do each day is incredible to me. And not only is it possible, it's really very simple. If I can do it, anyone can.

For seventeen years I languished in a full-time corporate position. I wasn't happy and I was barely making ends meet. I was thousands of dollars in debt and it was only getting worse. It wasn't the life I wanted. I felt that my life was just ticking away. When I sat down and really faced things, I knew in the end I could actually retire poor. Something had to be done.

Real estate investing came to me in the form of an infomercial at 2 a.m. on a Tuesday. The course piqued my interest, but the cost was $159. Money was so tight, I didn't have $159, but I did have a credit card and the company offered a 30-day money back guarantee. I held that credit card in my hand and considered the future I wanted. Then I picked up the phone and ordered the course. It was the first step toward a brand new life and eventual wealth beyond what I could have imagined.

But that was only the beginning. After a few years, I took a second step that propelled my business and my life to a whole new level. In 2001, when I quit my corporate job and took the plunge full-time into the world of real estate, I was immediately faced with a very big problem. It turns out that this problem was the best thing that could have happened to me. You see, without full-time employment, traditional lenders weren't exactly eager to loan me funds. And without consistently available money to fuel my real estate transactions, I had no business at all. I tried everything:

- Banks
- Line of credit
- Hard money lenders
- Partners
- Credit cards

If only I had known that all of these methods, even if they had been eager to give me a loan, were complete wastes of my time!

Finally, about five years ago I learned a lesson I'll never forget. I came across a foreclosure on a $150,000 property that was going for only $70,000. I'd hit the jackpot! It was almost too good to be true. Of course I jumped at the chance to get in on this incredible deal. But I didn't have the available funds. It's every real estate dealer's nightmare. I scrambled to the bank, to my partner. I tried to extend lines of credit. But all of this took time, and time is exactly what you don't have with a lucrative short sale like this.

As you can guess, I didn't get the sale. By the time I had secured funds, the property was sold to someone who had the cash ready and could close within days. In this one deal I lost a potential $60,000.

I swore then and there that this would never happen to me again. And it never did, because then I discovered private lending.

A whole new world opened to me and my investing has never been the same. Private lenders literally provide you with your own private bank to fund your real estate deals. Imagine: limitless funds that are constantly and immediately available. Today, I have more available capital than I do property in which to invest it. It's simply a store of money waiting for me to make use of it. And anyone can have this — that's what's so amazing. It's like a dream come true for any serious investor.

It sounds a little overwhelming, doesn't it? Let's slow down. I'll explain the specifics of private lending, and you'll see for yourself how this incredible system works.

Who are Private Lenders?

First of all, private lenders are everyday people. Some are retired, some work, some have substantial investment capital, and others have only a little. They may want to make the most of the savings they've spent their lives building, or perhaps they suddenly came into money through an inheritance or property sale. Regardless of their background, all private lenders are looking for a safe, high-yield opportunity for their funds. I give my lenders a guaranteed 10–15% return on their investment.

There's nothing like it anywhere. The incredible thing is that most people don't know about this opportunity. They let their hard-earned money sit in CD's or IRA's. Some even risk the volatile stock market. The win-win reality of private lending is unparalleled. Really, you get immediate, limitless funds to invest in real estate opportunities at a moment's notice.

Your lenders get an incredible 15% simple interest on their money. They are secured by both a mortgage and hazard insurance on the home. The safety of their investment is guaranteed because the total investment is never more than 70% of the appraised value of the property. Your lender can't lose. If for some reason you would fail to repay the loan, they have the value of the property to reclaim their funds. Not a bad deal for your lenders. Now, how does all of this work for you?

Why Use Private Lenders?

The advantage of using private lenders is truly staggering.

- Speed. The two greatest competitive advantages in the real estate market are cash-flow and speed. With private lending, you will already have your investors in place. When an opportunity arises, you have immediate funds to take action. What an incredible feeling to have the confidence that you'll never let another profitable opportunity slip away.
- Cash-flow. Because most lenders prefer not to deal with monthly payments, you have an ever-increasing flow of cash to use to your best advantage and that of your investor.
- Great deals on houses. We all know that cash upfront means a better deal on a home. Especially with short sales. Not only will you win a house out from under someone waiting on a bank loan, you'll pay less for the house as well!
- Close more deals. Immediate funds mean shorter transaction periods and more time to place money into new deals.
- No down payments.
- No pre-payment penalty.
- Reduced closing costs.
- No points like you'd have with mortgage brokers.
- You set the rules. For the first time, you'll be in control of your loans. In my business, I give 15% and no early withdrawal penalty, but when borrowing from a private lender, you can set any parameters you like. I use the generous terms because my lenders are very happy and come back to me over and over. I'm equipped with funds 100% of the time to take advantage of any deal which may arise. And, because of their involvement, I'm making a lot of money.

Where Do You Find Private Lenders?

Everywhere. I'll be honest, my very first private lender was my mother. She invested with me and, because she was living off the money, I sent her the interest checks

19

every month. Many lenders prefer to let the money sit and receive payment either quarterly or in one lump sum at the end. For them, this means something very similar to compound interest, except with a very high interest rate! And for you it means more funds accruing more revenue.

Find anyone with money stored in a CD or the stock market, and you'll have found a potential private lender. Think about it. Like all of us, private lenders want to make money. They seek safe, high-yield opportunities for their funds. CD's and money markets offer limited profits. Smart real estate investing offers them a return that is far and away above anything they are currently earning.

Methods of Finding Lenders Include:

- Family members and friends
- Newspaper ads
- Flyers
- Seminars
- Word of mouth.

Perhaps the most unexpected aspect of using private lenders is the accumulative response by satisfied lenders. After my first seminar I got only a few responses, at first. Then came the steady, unending trickle of eager lenders. Today, that trickle is more like a river! Maybe it's the credibility of one investor to another, or the proof of another's prosperity through investing, but word of mouth is so powerful that once you've established a few private lenders, you'll have a continual revenue stream with which to invest.

Real estate guru Ron LeGrand says, "There's plenty of capital out there. All you have to do is ask, and make people understand what you're using it for and how safe they are. It's really not difficult to get it." Simply educate lenders about the high rate of return available through your real estate investments, and watch them line up to give you money!

Incredible, I know. But listen to this: here are a few of my recent deals, made possible only because I had the cash on hand to close these deals quickly.

- Short Sale: $59,900 bank discounted to $25,000 = net $32,900
- Rehab: $51,000 purchased for $15k plus $13k rehab = net $23,207
- Subject to: $85,000 for $71,000 + $1,264 repairs = net $12,736
- Wholesale: $28,000 purchased for $22,000 = net $6,000

That's $74,843 in only four deals, and all because I had the confidence and flexibility of assured funds through private lenders.

Today I shake my head at the thought of it, but once upon a time I was practically begging for bank loans — for the opportunity to wait in line, fill out applications, and wait weeks or even months to see if they would deem me and my prospective property a good "risk."

I could have been using private lenders years earlier, but I hesitated. I lacked confidence and I wasn't sure where to start. If I could give one piece of advice to any budding investor it would be this: Start today.

Don't let even one more deal pass you by. You never know where life is going to take you. That one, 2 a.m. infomercial started me on this path, and today I'm the one appearing in the infomercials, teaching people how to change their lives through real estate.

With private lenders in line, you're always equipped with the funds you need to grab each opportunity as it arises. Your confidence will soar and you'll be making the kind of money of which you've always dreamed.

Private lending allowed me to finally take control of my destiny. You'll gain nothing by waiting. Discover the key to true freedom and big money in real estate investing. Private lenders are out there. They're waiting … .

Alan Cowgill is a speaker, author and real estate entrepreneur. Alan has bought or sold over 100 investment properties. His step-by-step system "Private Lending Made Easy" teaches others to find private lenders. Contact Alan at 937-390-6299. For a FREE audio go to www.PrivateLendingMadeEasy.com.

The One Year Freedom Plan

Master Real Estate's 13 Mental Assets and Quit Your Job in Just One Year

by Dave Hilgendorf

Have you had enough of trading hours for dollars? Does it bother you that you're making someone ELSE rich? Do you long to determine your own destiny and no longer leave it subject to factors beyond your control?

Back in 1999, I answered YES to all those questions. I had a job I enjoyed as a chemical engineer with a good salary, but wasn't happy. Before I was done reading the first page of my first real estate course, I knew I wanted to quit my job within one year, and did just that. I will never work for someone else again.

Since becoming a full-time real estate investor, I have bought and sold over 100 houses, wholesaling some to other investors, rehabbing and selling to owner occupants through new financing, owner financing and lease options, and keeping some as rentals. Things have worked out well for me, but if I did it over again, I would not have quit my job in one year. Quitting before I was fully ready made the challenge of running a business full-time without a steady income much harder than it needed to be. I don't want you to make the same mistake.

What *Don't* You Need to Quit Your Job in One Year?

- Experience
- A college degree
- Good credit
- A high net worth
- A lot of money
- Good looks
- Above average intelligence

What *Do* You Need?

- A strong dissatisfaction with your current situation (this is the leverage you need to motivate you).

"Know Your Purpose" A Powerful WHY!

- A powerful "WHY" — As Tony Robbins says, you need to know your purpose right from the start and it has to be a powerful reason for you. Without it you'll never succeed because you won't ever know what success means to you.
- A commitment to succeed — this has to be 100%, not 99%.
- An open mind — forget about what your parents or your co-workers think about your interest in real estate; you need to think differently than the way you're used to thinking and certainly differently from conventional wisdom.
- A positive attitude — this will remind you to have fun and enjoy the process.
- Discipline — this will get you through the tough times.
- Most of all, *YOU NEED A PLAN.* "You Need A PLAN"

You'll notice that the first six items on your list of requirements to quit your job have to do with your personal development, your character, your state of mind. These are about how you think about yourself, how well you know what you want in life, and how prepared and committed you are mentally, emotionally, physically and spiritually to your success. This is your foundation and is absolutely critical to your success.

What I lacked sufficiently during my year leading up to quitting my job, and what I've found to be the key ingredient to setting yourself up for success, was the right plan. You need a roadmap to follow so that once you know WHAT you want to achieve and WHY, you'll know exactly HOW to make it happen.

200 years ago, Ben Franklin developed a process to achieve a perfect moral character in just one year's time. Ben knew that perfection wasn't a realistic goal, but he also knew that aiming high would get him farther along toward his goal.

He identified 13 character traits critical for a perfect moral character. He resolved to focus on one trait each week. At the end of 13 weeks, he repeated the process. By the end of one year, he had intensely focused on each trait four separate times, improving each time on the previous week.

I have found that Franklin's process is an effective model for a strategic process I've developed to give the new investor maximum results in his or her first year effort to build a real estate business that can replace their current job. I call this process

"The One Year Freedom Plan"

Whether or not you learn it now the easy way, or years later the hard way, you will eventually find that there are approximately 13 areas of knowledge critical to your success in real estate. I call them "Mental Assets" since they are just as important as the real estate assets you will be buying, selling, and renting.

You need breadth and depth when it comes to these 13 Mental Assets. You need to learn them all, and you need to learn them well. By focusing on one trait intently for one full week at a time, you will force yourself to take the most important steps toward excelling in that particular area. Following in the proper order is the way that gives you the best chance to succeed.

Your year is divided into four separate sections of 13 weeks each. Each section has a different purpose in your quest. Think of this process like building a house:

1st 13 Weeks — Laying the foundation (learning the basic concepts)
2nd 13 Weeks — Building the frame (taking bold action, doing your first deals)
3rd 13 Weeks — Installing systems (learning from mistakes, solidifying systems)
4th 13 Weeks — Finishing touches (thinking and acting like a pro)

Here are Your 13 Mental Assets.

1. Understanding the different opportunities in real estate and the value of focusing on wholesaling and retailing your first year: You need to understand the basic exit strategies available to you before going into any deal, including wholesaling, retailing, renting, lease options, and owner financing. This will allow you to maximize every one of your resources and will prevent you from throwing away deals due to a lack of knowledge. Your first year, however, you need to be focused on creating chunks of cash through wholesaling and retailing and getting good at doing so consistently and predictably. You're replacing your current job with a buy/sell machine. You can get sophisticated later.

2. Having effective communication and negotiation skills: As Ron LeGrand says, flapping your lips is the highest paid profession in the world. This is most critical when you're dealing one-on-one with sellers, but is just as important with buyers, contractors, attorneys, realtors, insurance agents, and everyone else who will be helping you reach your goals. Listening to people and understanding what they want and figuring out how to most effectively provide that to them — while simultaneously achieving your objective — is an advanced and absolutely essential skill. Mastering this Mental Asset will make you and others you touch rich in the wallet as well as in the soul.

3. Developing, tracking, and achieving your goals: There's a lot of information available on goal setting. You need goals that inspire passion and stretch you. First you develop a vision, then you back track to how you're going to reach your vision.

Dev A Vision   (How To REACH Your Vision)

4. Getting, keeping, and maintaining good credit: This is not critical the first year when you're primarily wholesaling and retailing houses. However, once you start keeping rental properties and building passive income that will eventually set you free, your credit counts big time and creates opportunities for you that you won't want to — and may not be able to afford to — miss out on. If you don't have good credit, you need to learn the art of fixing it, improving it, and maintaining it. This is an ongoing process, not a one-time event.

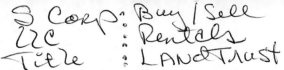

Handwritten at top: S Corp: Buy/Sell LLC : Rentals Title : Land Trust

5. Understanding Asset Protection: You need to know and be able to implement the basics. You can worry about getting more complicated later. Set up your S-corporation for buying and selling. Form an LLC for keeping rentals. Take title to each property you buy in a Land Trust to maintain privacy on public records. Be honest and fair with people to avoid lawsuits.

6. Understanding money: You will need to know how to find it (private money, hard money, credit cards, equity lines, local banks) to fund your purchases. You have to understand how to use it most effectively and smartly. Cash flow is the gasoline that runs your small business engine. Learn how to avoid, eliminate, and manage consumer debt

7. Building Your Wealth Team: You won't make it without them. First identify all team members and the criteria you will look for in each of them. Then, go out and find them. Be willing to change any of your team members when they are not up to your standards. Always have a backup for each team member.

8. Marketing effectively to sellers: You need to work only with motivated sellers and only with proven direct response marketing techniques. Understanding how to systemize this process will make you RICH. You can't rely on any one "magic bullet." You need to be able to put a lot of lines in the water at all times and never stop the buying machine.

9. Understanding the cost of home repairs and how to effectively work with contractors: Learn how to quickly and accurately estimate repairs on houses so you can make offers with confidence. You need to know where to find the best contractors and understand the "contractor triangle" and how to use it to your advantage. Comprehend how to never let them get them ahead of you on draws. and how to stay on schedule.

10. Constructing offers that guarantee minimum profits: This is not a guessing game; you need a proven formula so you know your exit before you enter. In your first year when you're wholesaling and retailing, you will primarily be making all cash offers with no contingencies. You will need to buy cheap enough to build in your required profit along with the unexpected expenses.

11. Marketing effectively to buyers: Whether you are wholesaling to investors, retailing to new homeowners, or finding renters, some basic strategies are consistent. You need to generate a lot of leads through signs, newspaper ads, MLS listings, and flyers. You need to allow the buyers to get the information they need to decide if they are interested without taking your time. Once someone raises a hand, you need to prescreen them quickly and act quickly.

12.Effective Property Management: This is not as critical your first year, but you need to start learning the basics of good property management before you buy your first rental property. It starts with the pre-screening process and knowing what to look for. Setting the tone up front with your renter is important with a solid rental agreement and a mutual understanding of expectations. Your goal is to keep your tenant as long as possible while still maintaining market rent.

13. Learning to delegate tasks and focus on high revenue activities: As your skills develop, you will need to make sure the nature of your activities stays consistent with those new skills. As you think of and treat your business as a real business, you will get out of the mode of "doing" everything, and instead learn to lead and manage the process. You shouldn't be swinging a hammer, sticking stamps on postcards, or walking around with your cell phone permanently attached to your ear.

Each week, you should focus on one of these Assets. During the 1st 13 weeks (the foundation stage), your job is to understand the basic concepts behind every one of these tools and be fully prepared to hit the ground running in a big way the next go around. You need to learn from those that have walked before you during this time. Don't try to reinvent the wheel. For free tips on what to focus on your first 13 weeks, go to www.quitin1year.com.

During the 2nd 13 weeks (the framing stage), it's time to take action, and I mean massive action. You need to make bold steps in every category. You need to do a bare minimum of three deals (two wholesale deals and one retail deal) during this period of time.

During the 3rd 13 weeks (the systems stage), it's time to get serious about this as a business. It's time to reflect on what you learned during the 2nd stage and reassess your commitment to your goal of quitting in one year. You also need to solidify the systems you have in every category. You will also do a minimum additional three wholesale deals and two retail deals.

During the 4th set of 13 weeks (finishing touches) you need to start acting and feeling like a pro. You need to imagine in everything you do in the business, in all 13 areas, that you have already gone full-time. You'll do at least three wholesale deals and two retail deals.

You may be asking at this point, when the end of one year comes around …

How Will I Know If Should Quit My Job?

Good question! It's an even better question if you ask it at the beginning of this one year process instead of at the end. If you know where you need to be, you can track your progress along the way and make adjustments if necessary.

To confidently quit your job, you should be able to check off every item on this list. (These are guidelines; depending on your risk threshold, you may modify these up or down.)

- Budget established — you need to know how much you and your family need to live each month and how much your business needs to survive each month, and you need to know it with confidence

- Cash reserves — a minimum of three months of personal and business expenses in reserves (in the bank, in a separate account from your operating account)

- Credit lines — preferably a minimum of $50,000 in available credit through credit cards, equity lines, etc.

- Good credit — your beacon score should be a minimum of 650, 680 if possible.

- Minimal debt — you should have less than $30,000 in consumer debt (credit card balances, auto loan, etc.)

- You need a minimum of two private or hard money sources identified with a minimum of $200,000 total cash available.

- A minimum of six wholesale deals completed with a minimum gross profit (before tax) of $6,000 each.

- You need a primary and backup person in whom you have confidence for every one of your wealth team members

- A minimum of three retail deals completed with a minimum gross profit each of $15,000 each.

- A minimum of two rental properties, each one providing a net cash flow after PITIM (principal, interest, taxes, insurance, and maintenance) of $200/month.

- Personal commitment and resolve — you have to be passionate about this thing and absolutely certain about your commitment to see it through.

- You need to have your S-corp set up for your buy and sell business and an LLC established for your keeper properties, with checking accounts set up for each.

If you have not met every one of these criteria at a level with which you are comfortable, you should not quit your job. The best way to make sure you will be ready in one year is to set goals for yourself along the way.

Divide each of the criteria above by four and set for yourself "13 Week Goals" to make sure you're heading in the right direction.

Obviously, how successful you are in achieving your goals will depend not just on what you do during the year but where you start out. The more solid ground you are when you start, the better your chance of success.

But remember, no matter where you are financially, physically, or emotionally, the best way for you to reach your financial goals is through real estate, and the best time to get started in real estate is *NOW*.

I firmly believe that ANYONE can quit their job in one year with the right plan no matter what their current situation is, but NO ONE will be able to do so if they don't get started TODAY.

Dave Hilgendorf is a full time real estate investor specializing in wholesaling and retailing single family homes. He publishes a weekly e-newsletter where he gives free advice for investors at all levels. Dave is passionate about sharing his experiences with others and helping people get started in the real estate business "the right way" so they can quit their job within one year and do so with confidence and a high chance of success. If you would like to get more detailed information on the 13 Mental Assets and how to set up your one-year plan to quit your job, or if you want to order your FREE Report entitled "Your First 13 Weeks, Learning The Critical Skills to Succeed in Real Estate and Quit Your Job in One Year," *contact Dave Hilgendorf at www.quitin1year.com, e-mail him at dave@quitin1year.com, call him at 912-844-5512, or write to him at PO Box 30718, Savannah, GA 31410.*

The Road to INCREDIBLE WEALTH .
The Street Smart Way!

How to Create Massive Passive Cash Flow in Real Estate

by Louis "Lou" Brown

I love real estate, and it has made me and my family very comfortable. It has provided a beautiful home, nice cars, incredible vacations and a lifestyle that most people would love to have. In my 28 years of investing, I've learned a thing or two about making huge piles of money. No doubt about it: real estate is the ideal investment **for massive passive cash!**

In order for you to make the most money possible, you need a proven strategy for creating wealth that is simple, easy to follow and fool proof. Over the years I've created a ***Street Smart Wealth System.*** Here I'll share its accelerated income and wealth proven key points that generate incredible wealth.

The system starts at the very beginning: finding the best deals and negotiating them in order to provide the best short term and long term benefits. After negotiation and acquisition, you must get the most long-term profit the right way. The system walks through finding occupants who take care of your property, who get up in the morning and go to work so you don't have to. For that, you need a plan. My system includes how you can …

- Uncover deals no one else knows about
- Finance those deals without having to go to the bank
- Purchase them privately so you don't reveal your real estate holdings to the world
- Correctly renovate or repair the property without the typical hassles, contractor problems and expense others experience
- Find the right tenants to "hire" for your property
- Appear as a professional property manager, not the owner
- Super charge your cash flow to generate "massive passive income" to allow you to get free of the shackles of your current job

Creating your Wealth Strategy

Too often would-be investors hear of someone else's success and take various uninformed stabs at trying to duplicate it. Usually they stampede ahead with no real plan for success or protection against known pitfalls. That stunts growth, many times leading to failure and abandonment of this great investment vehicle. I'll show you how you can do it right. Better than that, I'll show you how to go further faster. My *"Street Smart"* methods of real estate investing bypass the traditional ways investment real estate is typically located, negotiated, purchased, managed and sold. I believe you should establish a plan for wealth (Get a free copy of the **Street Smart Wealth System** wheel by going to www.louisbrown.com).

Buy Right/Buy Cheap

Your plan should include a system. Here's the most fantastic wealth building system I've found for the average person to catapult their profit-making potential into the stratosphere. It's a system to **Buy Right,** buying as cheaply as possible, using checklists to determine the best possible offers based on the situation of the seller. Usually someone who plans to buy property gets with a realtor, looks at a few properties, makes an offer a few percent below asking price, and then goes to the bank and qualifies for a new 30-year loan. Forget that nonsense! That is not my plan for you to achieve higher than average returns and extra income that sets you free financially.

Get Instant Equity

My plan uses nontraditional ways to find and buy that meet the **Instant Equity** goal of your wealth strategy. This system includes many unique ways to generate incoming and outgoing leads. An example of an incoming lead is someone calling you as a result of an ad you place in the newspaper. An outgoing lead generator is a marketing letter or postcard you send to folks in foreclosure.

To maximize results, this system includes making offers that avoid banks. I've been able to buy many millions of dollars' worth of single family and small multi-family properties over the last three decades, without once qualifying for a traditional loan. Your system should include unique ways to buy without banks, such as taking over the seller's existing financing and having the seller carry back financing. Every offer should be carefully crafted to meet the seller's needs (not wants).

Generating Income

Once your property is purchased, the plan goes on to tenant selection to accomplish the Income goal of this IDEAL investment. Some investors are terrified at the thought of Property Management. That fear is unfounded when legitimate issues are addressed. First, don't be the owner — be the manager. Proper property management involves protecting you from a confrontation with a tenant who doesn't do as agreed. One way we accomplish this is to have the property owned by a Trust, not by you. The trust hires you as the manager via a Management Agreement. By this approach, you must clear anything outside the Rental Agreement with the owner. I advise that the "owner" not agree to anything outside the agreement. Remember, our goal is to have a system that provides you an above average income stream with few hassles.

Profit Centers

Dependable monthly income sets you free. Having a series of built-in *Profit Centers* increases your cash flow and accelerates your wealth. My system includes many … Pet Fees, Pet Rent, Extra person fees, Additional rent, Discounted rent and more.

Another "Income Accelerator" involves offering potential renters the option to buy the property. Why would I do this? It's another profit center/problem solver. We sell them the chance to buy. That's a very powerful attraction to someone who wants to get ahead. And we offer them a great deal, too — including partial rent credits toward the purchase, credit of their initial (non-refundable) option consideration and even back up owner financing. My experience is that we end up with a better tenant who typically improves our property. Imagine that! Many do not exercise the option to buy for various personal reasons, which is probably why they are tenants. Oh, well! You end up getting a better property back and starting over!

The option wealth and cash flow accelerator gives you the benefit of non-refundable option fees, a better property and better tenants. If they do buy you get the price you want, they pay the closing costs, no realtors fees, and you get rent right up to the date of closing and more! Can it get any better than that? Yes! The strategy goes on to have you offer to carry back the home financing. Why kill the Goose that lays the Golden Egg? We offer to carry under a concept called "Agreement for Deed." It works sort of like vehicle financing, where the lender keeps the title until you pay them off. Here you keep the Deed (control) until your buyer pays you off. With this strategy you get extra income, because they must pay at least 10% down to get the owner-financing plan in our "American Dream Homeownership Program." You receive interest income, and you just might end up getting the house back … just like a bank. If you can't beat 'em, join 'em!

Tax Benefits/Retirement Accelerators

Under the rental/option scenario we get to accomplish another goal: *Tax Benefits* through the excess depreciation the government gives us for being landlords. Are you starting to see the *Retirement Accelerators* that come from receiving the Option fees and the Down Payments? There is so much more profit available to us. Because you have a plan and a system, you'll be able to earn all these profit centers from each house. It just doesn't take many to get really wealthy.

The process of buying right, keeping as many as you can by buying the right way, managing right by including the profit centers, avoiding taxes, and holding right using Land and Personal Property Trusts to *Avoid Lawsuits and Probate* combine to create a winning formula of profit centers that is unbeatable when applied right. In order to accomplish this you need the right paperwork and training designed to produce all these benefits. For this and more on the Wealth System go to: www.louisbrown.com

Why Real Estate Is I.D.E.A.L.

By *holding whenever possible rather than selling* you receive advantages that are unparalleled against *any other* investment strategy. Having money work for you instead of you working for it is the I.D.E.A.L. investment.

"I" = Income

Income is an important element of any good investment … without it you have to carry costs such as taxes, insurance and any interest expense out of your own pocket. When you rent to someone else, they pay all those costs plus a return on your investment. But here's the big news … your income is hedged against inflation. As the value of the dollar declines and prices rise, so does your rental income. If you have fixed costs such as interest on the loan, then you get the benefit of paying back the debt with deflating dollars while your income goes up.

"D" = Depreciation

Couple this with a formidable tax strategy that allows us as investors to pretend, for tax purposes, that the value of our property is going down while we really know that in most areas it is going up. We are receiving tax benefits (*Depreciation*) while receiving income. The income exceeds our expenses, yet we get to write off more than our income. This results in tax losses. Uncle Sam tells us that we lose money even though we made money. I think they call that "Voodoo Economics." Of course, the real reason the government allows us these tax incentives is to entice us to invest in rental real estate. They learned they aren't very good landlords and decided giving the public an incentive to deal with tenants would help get them out of the landlording business. So this means you can own it, "lose money" while making money, use the "losses" to offset other income and actually zero out your taxes! Imagine that. But it gets even better!

"E" = Equity

Another benefit is the pay-down of the mortgage over time. You don't actually pay off the loan — the tenants do! Every month you receive rent and make a payment on the loan, you are putting money in the bank as principle pay-down of the loan. I call my houses "banks." What better place to keep the *Equity* build up than in those individual banks spread out in different neighborhoods? But there's still more.

"A" = Appreciation

Historically real estate has gone up in value over time. This Appreciation is somewhat predictable depending on the area of the country in which you live. In almost any case, you can force appreciation through improving the property. Real estate appreciation is what most folks point to as their foundation of lifetime wealth. But they are usually referring to the one property they own — the house they live in. What if you had several houses and/or apartments? That would grow your wealth faster and farther. But we're not finished yet!

"L" = Leverage

Then comes the icing on the cake. Not only can you receive income, write off more than you make, and let the tenants pay down the mortgage as the property increases in value, but you get a huge bonus. *Leverage*. Bankers allow the public to borrow 80-90 even 100 percent of the value of the real estate. Why is that? Because they understand that real estate is safe collateral to lend money against. It has traditionally held its value and is very forgiving in that if it were to drop in value, it is a very slow drift which usually comes back in line quickly.

Contrast that with the stock market. Do you know what the brokerage houses will lend on a stock? Usually 50% of value. That's 50% leverage in stocks vs. up to 100% in real estate. What do the stockbrokers know? Stocks are risky. Stocks can lose huge value quickly and are slow to forgive. Leverage gives you the opportunity to invest little to none of your own money and control an income-producing asset with excess tax benefits as it grows in value while the user (your tenant) pays off the debt. There … now go find me something better.

A lot of long time investors will tell you that the best you can expect from your rental investment portfolio over time is about a 10% return. Well for most of us 10% compounded over many years will do just fine. I'm sure a lot of you wish you could say that about your investments in the stock market. But what they don't know is you can add a system to make it better than average.

The secrets those long-term investor/landlords don't know about are Cash Flow and Retirement Accelerators. These are strategically-placed profit centers I have added to the income stream of our rental investment portfolio. Those who make a modest return can easily triple that with the formulas from the *Street Smart Wealth Strategy.*

An integrated plan with processes to incorporate all the various profits and avoid as many pitfalls as possible is the key to your success. Such a plan exists. It's the culmination of three decades of proven concepts that have not only worked for me but for thousands of students in all 50 states, Canada and ten foreign countries. It's the "whole enchilada" of real estate investing. It's designed to extract the most profit from every acquisition and sale, plus the most profit and least aggravation while holding the assets.

Use this plan for wealth that contains the step-by-step guidance of a completely integrated and interlaced system of concepts as well as the tools to implement the actions required to get the money. Good luck while getting financially free!

Louis "Lou" Brown draws from a wide and varied background as a real estate investor. He's invested in single-family homes, apartments, and hotels, developed subdivisions and built and renovated homes and apartments. Being a teacher at heart, he enjoys sharing his discoveries with others. Husband, Father, Author, Lecturer, Inventor, Investor, Builder, Designer and Real Estate expert are all descriptions of this exciting trainer. Go to www.louisbrown.com or call 1-800-578-8580 to get more training, articles, e-zine subscription, and the latest cutting edge tools for successful real estate investing.

The Ten Generalized Principles of
Active Investing

by John R. Burley

Beyond being an author and financial educator and an active investor, I have earned my place in the arena of successful investors by focusing on creating wealth through innovative real estate strategies. Over the past several years, I have closed deals on a weekly basis that have literally created tens of thousands of dollars of profit per deal. One of the keys to my success as an active investor has been following a set of ten generalized principles. By sticking to these principles in my investing endeavors, I have been able to consistently achieve personal and financial success. In this chapter, I would like to share those principles with you in the hope that you too, will discover your own financial prosperity.

-FAITH
BELIEF
ACTION

The Ten Generalized Principles of Investing

The 1st Generalized Principle of Active Investing is 'Believe.' After comparing those who are successful long-term investors with those who aren't, I discovered that successful people all started with, or soon gained a belief that what they were doing would work. Belief is a key ingredient in stepping out into the world of successful investing. Belief precedes action. Investors pursue a course of action, because they believe that their actions will produce great financial results. Active investors are people who believe that they can reach their financial goals and experience the freedom that comes from controlling their own destinies. When it comes to developing an investment strategy, active investors believe in themselves and their ability to make it happen. As you take steps to become an active investor, let your first step be a step of faith. Believe in yourself and your ideas.

"BELIEVE IN Yourself + Your IdEAS"

The 2nd Generalized Principle of Active Investing is 'Do What You Love and Love What You Do.' Ask yourself what area of investing appeals to you in a way that really grabs and keeps your attention? With very few exceptions, successful investors are very passionate about their work. They thoroughly enjoy their working hours and often treat their businesses and investments with the care they would treat a child who needs nurturing in order to grow and prosper.

35

The 3rd Generalized Principle of Active Investing is 'Determine Your Niche.' I cannot stress enough how critical it is that you do this. Without exception, every millionaire I know can tell you in a couple of sentences exactly what it is they do that has made them so successful and rich! Without a precise knowledge of what you do, your chances for success are greatly diminished. Keep in mind that your niche can always be adjusted. If you decide you don't like the "game" you are playing, you can change your niche and take your ball to a game you like.

The 4th Generalized Principle of Active Investing is 'Become a Master of Leverage.' You must leverage your own time and constantly focus on how you can access the skills, time, resources and money of other people. Leveraging resources is the most valuable tool available to the active investor for compounding investment returns and accelerating the process of wealth building.

Mastering your leverage of time will involve three main disciplines:

- Allocate at least 10 quality hours per week to concentrate on your investment strategies.

- Learn to prioritize your time in favor of the important and challenging tasks that bring you the most wealth. Remember that usually about 15-20% of what you do brings about 80% of your income.

- Learn the most efficient use of your prioritized time so that you get more important work done in less time. This will involve task delegations to other people who have particular areas of expertise that exceed yours, and systems streamlining.

Mastering the leverage of other people's skills will involve assembling a team of experts who support and counsel you to assist you in meeting your objectives. You cannot be a successful investor without the assistance and expertise of other people.

The 5th Generalized Principle of Active Investing is 'Think Laterally.' Lateral thinking is the art of looking at things from different points of view. You can make a lot of money by doing very simple things that other people have overlooked. In simple terms, ask yourself how could something be done better or what do people want that they are not getting now?

As an active investor, I apply lateral thinking by providing the opportunity for the average non-home owner to own a home. I firmly believe that the best way to make a lot of money is to help a lot of people in a significant way. I do this without exploitation. Close to 25% of the population would like to own their own home but cannot do so using conventional means of financing. I relieve their pain by providing them with a housing opportunity. This is an example of lateral thinking within my niche of real estate investing.

Opportunity for non home owner to own a home.

The 6th Generalized Principle of Active Investing is 'Do Market Research.'
As you progress in "The Game" you will become a master of your market. Keep in mind that, while market research is important, the only way to become a master of your market is to actually be in the market. Jump in and learn as much as you can while playing the game. Remember, if you need to know everything before starting, you will never get started. You must avoid analysis paralysis.

The 7th Generalized Principle of Active Investing is 'Be Efficient.' One of the hardest things for poor and middle-class people to understand is that hard work and money have very little to do with each other. Mastering efficiency depends very much on understanding the principle of leverage: having people, time, resources and money working for you and not against you.

Hard-work & money have little to do with Each other.

All successful investment strategies feature streamlined systems that allow the investor to accomplish more with less effort and less time. Ideally they are run so efficiently that they continue to run whether or not the investor is directly overseeing them on a regular basis. I cannot stress enough the importance of systems. My business and real estate investing is designed so that an "average" person could come in and run it indefinitely. I do, however, continually improve my systems by engaging "exceptional" people to run the show.

The 8th Generalized Principle of Active Investing is 'Let Lag Work.' The time-honored principle of lag is best described by the biblical theme that you "reap what you sow." In other words, if you follow the principles outlined in this chapter and persist, you will be successful. The benefits follow the labor. The 'reaping what you sow' theme has two implications. It refers not only to the effort you make, but also to the character or quality of the effort. An element of "what goes around comes around" is carried in the concept of lag.

When handed a setback, rather than giving into fear and quitting, bolster your determination to meet the challenge and keep going. If your principles are sound, then all you have to do is make minor adjustments until you find your own formula for success. Adjust your strategy until it is a good fit for the ten generalized principles. Lag guarantees your success if you will just get in the game and stay there. Keep the faith, persist and you will be rewarded.

The 9th Generalized Principle of Active Investing is 'Understand Timing.'
Windows of opportunity exist in every market. It is just a matter of using lateral thinking and market research to locate and recognize them. So look around your market. Find the opportunities and jump in!

The key to proper timing is to ensure that your niche fits into the timing of your market — that you are not selling straw hats in the winter, only buying. Be prepared to modify or adapt your niche if the timing in your market is wrong for your first choice of strategy. Your market research will identify the timing issue

37

for you. Do not get hung up on the idea that there is only one way to be a successful investor.

The 10th Generalized Principle of Active Investing is 'Take Action.' Rich people are masters of action. They understand that the only way to find the right formula for success is to participate in the game. Poor people are masters of excuses. They lay blame on others and on circumstances. Their fears provide them with an endless babbling stream of seemingly logical reasons why they cannot and should not act. This negative internal chatter is simply psycho-babble. You and only you are responsible for your success or failure. Take action!

These ten principles have guided my investment career. They have been major tools that I have used to carve out my personal financial freedom. My hope is that you will apply the Ten Generalized Principles of Investing to your investment strategies so you can enjoy the financial freedom that you deserve!

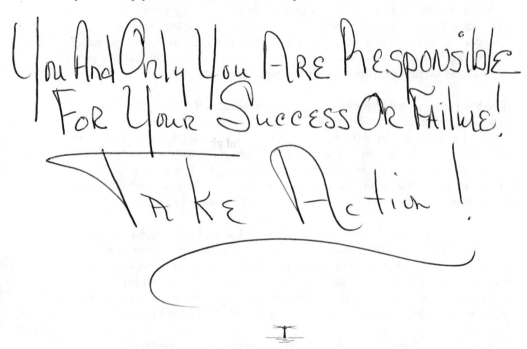

John Burley has completed over 1000 real estate transactions. John is a best-selling author, a sought-after financial educator and an internationally recognized authority on real estate investing. To learn more about John Burley's wealth creating strategies, books, audio courses, and seminars, visit his website at www.johnburley.com.

Wealth Secrets of Millionaires

by Peter Lowe

Many people think that becoming rich is an impossible dream. When they picture millionaire's, they think of big spenders living lavish, glamourous life-styles. The average millionaire is a very different sort of person.

According to financial consultant Todd Barnhart, the average self-made millionaire is a "middle-aged (or older) person who drives a moderately-priced car... Is married twenty years or more to the same person, goes to church... Owns or runs a business, has kids or grandkids, works ten hours a day and loves it." In other words, the typical American millionaire is an ordinary person who has achieved wealth and success over time, by working, planning and saving for it. You can do the same!

Our free enterprise system creates opportunities, and gives us the freedom to take advantage of them. No matter what your background, you can become a millionaire! These six secrets helped bring extraordinary success to seemingly ordinary people. They can do the same for you.

Secret 1: Treat Money as a Servant, Not as a Master

Jesus Christ said, "No one can serve two masters. You cannot serve both God and money." Money is a wonderful servant, but a terrible master.

Financial consultant Robert Ringer cautions in his book Million Dollar Habits, "Instead of possessing money, what happens when an individual's goal is money is that he becomes possessed by money. Instead of keeping money in perspective, it becomes an obsession."

An obsessive pursuit of riches can bring other problems: far too many people have sacrificed their health to gain wealth, only to spend their wealth trying to regain their health. A proper outlook on money is needed to become — and remain — healthy, wealthy and wise.

39

Secret 2: Form Wealthy Habits

Have you ever wondered how some people become wealthy so easily? No matter what they do, money seems to gravitate to them. They have learned the millionaire's secret of making a habit of making money. They live in such a way that making money becomes as natural and habitual as eating or sleeping. Todd Barnhart wrote in his book, The Five Rituals of Wealth, "I've found one thing to be absolutely true of those who control vast resources: they don't just do wealthy things once in a while when they feel like it. They habitually live in a state of wealth... They save, dream, plan, invest and give in a never-ending cycle."

What are the habits of wealth? I'm going to share with you the three most important habits you can adopt. They are simple, timeless, and unchanging. And they are the foundation of building wealth and financial security.

I. Spend less than you earn. The first habit of wealth is to make the best use of the financial resources you already have. No matter what your salary, you should make it a habit to spend less than you earn. Everyone can reduce their expenditures without making a significant dent in their lifestyles. If you doubt this, I challenge you to account for every dollar you spent last month. How much of it was necessary? How much was important? If you are like most people, doing a personal audit of your purchases for even one month will reveal that you spent a lot of money on things you didn't need, didn't really want, and may not even like.

II. Form a savings plan. The second habit of wealth goes hand-in-hand with the first. Once you get your spending under control, you can form a savings plan, and begin tracking your growing wealth. Wealth is measured by how much you keep, not how much you make. Every time you receive a paycheck, set aside a portion of it to keep — preferably, ten percent or more.

III. Invest your savings. The third habit of wealth is to make your money multiply by putting your savings to work through sound investments. Hoarding money will make you a miser, not a millionaire. The essence of investment is to generate wealth-creating opportunities for others and to share in the wealth created. The more, and more wisely, you invest, the more wealth you create for yourself and others.

Secret 3: Find Work You Love

I am convinced that the surest — and most fun! — way to succeed financially is to love your work. Most of America's millionaires made their fortune not by running after profit, but by throwing themselves into work they adored. They viewed their work as a mission, and riches became a byproduct.

One financial expert did a study of self-made millionaires to find out what set them apart from others. He concluded that the single most distinct quality about these wealthy individuals was their love of and absorption in their work. He stated, "Long before they knew whether they'd be paid enough to support themselves, they were caught up in their work and doing far more of it than they realized."

Secret 4: Set Goals

The famous multi-millionaire Napoleon Hill, who wrote down Andrew Carnegie's secrets to wealth in his best-seller Think and Grow Rich, put it this way: "There is one quality which one must possess to win, and that is definiteness of purpose, the knowledge of what one wants, and a burning desire to possess it."

Conversely, the failure to set goals is the surest route to financial failure. Indeed, the refusal to set goals is the surest route to financial failure. Indeed, the refusal to set clear, specific goals is the most common feature of the bankrupt and broke. According to one study, more than 95 percent of the people who consider themselves financial failures lack a financial plan.

Secret 5: Shun Shady Schemes

The quickest way to destroy your fortune and reputation is to engage in unwise or unethical deals and practices. No matter how wealthy you are, your wealth is never secure unless it has been built on a foundation of integrity. Many of the richest men in America — Ivan Boesky and Michael Milkin, for example — have seen their financial empires disintegrate overnight because of unethical practices. To keep your wealth safe and growing, build on a foundation of integrity.

Secret 6: Invest in Yourself Through Education

Investing in yourself not only brings high yields; it is invulnerable to inflation, impervious to recession, and totally unaffected by stock market crashes. Material possessions, stocks and bonds, and liquid assets can be stolen, lost or destroyed; but the sum of your wisdom, expertise and abilities are yours to keep forever. As the great entrepreneur Henry Ford stated, "If money is hope for independence, you will never have it. The only real security that a man can have... Is a reserve of knowledge, experience and ability." Another way to say it, is to earn more, you need to learn more.

Peter Lowe and his SUCCESS seminars have been featured in Time *magazine,* People *magazine, on the covers of* Selling! *and* Personal Selling Power *magazines,* USA Today, *on* ABC's 20/20, CBS This Morning, CNN *and on the front pages of every major newspaper from coast to coast.*

Turn the Rock Over:
Eight Strategies for Success in Real Estate

by Casey Kellar

For the last 28 years my husband and I have run multiple businesses and have developed real estate. In the early years, our manufacturing company was started with $5,000 cash (borrowed from my mother) and a $3,000 credit line on a credit card. We grew the company to millions in sales in less than two years. We are entrepreneurs, and have fun starting and running companies. Some of the companies we have built from the ground up are: a retail brand product marketed in the gift industry; a gift and antique store; a fitness center; an AFL/CIO entertainment agency; and a real estate development company.

Some of our businesses have been wildly successful, some just so-so. Some we kept, and others we sold. Most of our very best profits and cash flows have come from our real estate acquisitions and development businesses. It has been mentioned before by more than one wealthy individual that there are two primary strategies to gaining great wealth.

- Strategy 1 — To own your own company
- Strategy 2 — To buy real estate.

The reason for this is simple. You want the best tax advantages teamed with passive income which is what both of these strategies accomplish. What business or product do you think of when someone says "McDonald's"? The most usual response is "hamburgers." However, when a chief executive of McDonald's was asked this question, he replied, "We are in the real estate business." McDonald's buys the real estate for their franchises and then sells the "business" on a franchise.

Lesson one: Know what business you are in.

Our Top Eight Strategies for Success in Business and Real Estate Investing

No matter if it is a traditional/non-traditional business, or the business of real estate investing, these eight simple rules apply.

www.mentorsmagazine.com

1. Define yourself and your market. One of the most important things we learned right away was to treat our real estate investing as a business. The very first thing you need to do is to define both yourself and your business.

Begin your business with a business definition, goals, a working plan, and an exit strategy. When it comes to real estate, too many investors adopt the "throw it on the wall and see if it sticks" mentality.

There once was a man who was referred to me for an "emergency consult." He was in trouble and could not figure out what had gone wrong. He had taken several classes and was just at the end of his first year in real estate investing. During his first year he had bought and leveraged into: three individual houses, one mixed use commercial building, one 10-space mobile home park, one 24-unit apartment building, and one vacation rental. Quite an accomplishment for a beginner!

So I asked him … "Which business are you in?" He replied, "What do you mean? I'm in the real estate business!" There it was … his main problem was that he was just investing in real estate without a plan. I explained to him that there are several different real estate investment strategies such as: The pretty house business (buying new or pretty houses), the ugly house business (buying and rehab), commercial real estate, multi-family housing, etc … .

He needed to find what he knew best (which of course, was what he was having the most success at), sell the others and focus on getting experienced and wildly successful at that market first. Then and only then would it be okay for him to continue to learn something new and try it. He was a man of action, and I loved that, because that is what it takes to be successful. Unfortunately, on the concept of "divide and conquer," this guy had been his own worst enemy.

What was our solution to a happy ending? We discovered he was doing best with individual houses. This was what he understood best. He sold off the other properties, generated enough cash to get himself on his feet, and then continued to build his individual house purchase program until he was successful and skilled enough to move on.

The moral of this story: Start with one real estate system. Work it until you are comfortable/successful with it. Then it is okay to learn a new skill and move on.

When you buy or leverage, always know what business you are in, plan your work, work your plan and have an exit strategy in mind. It is your business, not just an investment.

We have no issue with rapid growth as long as you know what business you are in, put plans and systems in place, and insure there is adequate capitalization.

www.mentorsmagazine.com

2. Set up a system to run your real estate business. Most real estate investors do not consider their "investing" as a business. In step one you have defined what real estate business you are specializing in. Each investment property should be looked at as its own little business center with profits, losses, advertising, customers, etc. You need to treat each profit center (individual investment) as a "business within a business."

This way you can view which of your investments are worth keeping and which should be cut from the herd.

Interestingly enough, most people keep their losers and sell their winners. When we had a retail line in the gift industry, we were in the business of wholesaling a wide range of bath and beauty products to stores. One time I was making a follow up call to a store that had not re-ordered for a while. I asked the store's buyer how sales were going and how much inventory of our product she had on the shelf. She replied, "When we got the shipment, it sold so quickly, we have been out for some time." Confused, I asked why she did not order more. She told me she had so many other products on the shelves that were not selling that she was waiting until the other products sold. Then she would order more of ours. Sigh. You know the rest of the story. That store went out of business a few months later due to lack of cash flow. I see people doing the same thing in real estate. If they have something performing well, they hurry and take their profits out, but hold their poor performing properties, hoping that they will do better.

Sometimes you need to sell something to generate investment cash, but evaluate carefully to make sure you are not "holding losers" and selling all your winners and not replacing them. By making each property its own "small business" within your real estate investing business, you will be able to make clear and informed decisions knowing where your money is made, and where it is lost. It will also help you see overall cost and profit flow opportunities throughout all of your investments together as a business as well as individually. *Find a good business system, learn it and make it a part of what you do.*

3. "Turn the Rock" to find your business niche and generate more profits. A rock is creative. Just by being itself, it can be re-created. If you don't believe it, take a moment to think about this … the first wheel came from a rock. The concept of a "pet rock" sold for millions. A rock is solid. It is a great foundation to build on.

Our phrase "Turn The Rock" means "to look at something a different way, from a new perspective, to be creative — to find your market niche." Look at your competition. You do not have to re-invent the wheel, just give your wheel something special … like added value or service or some fun benefit that will make you stand out. In manufacturing when we turn the rock, I call it "product tweaking" but it works in real estate or any other industry. "Product tweaking" is simply borrowing an idea from another type of product or industry and seeing how it will work for the current product or project you are working on.

Break out of your mold or set pattern of thinking. Laugh and be silly. Sir Winston Churchill always had a twinkle in his eye and possessed a quick wit that was "timeless." A reporter once asked him, "What do you think is the secret to youth?" He replied, "Give up your childish ways, but ALWAYS maintain your CHILDLIKE qualities." I love this quote. Visualize with the eyes of youth. Look at things in a new way, or try a silly or unique approach. Find something that fills a need, a way to make something better for the customer, bank, anyone or anything — something to set you apart from the crowd. Then test market your idea. When you know you have a home run … run with it!

Ask yourself the following questions:
1. Who are your customers? (What kind of renters/purchasers for this property?)
2. Who is your competition? (Rental/sales comps for this property.)
3. Where does your "quality/price/business" fit against your competition? (Does it have or can you develop or capitalize on a special feature/change to make it worth more.)

List three things that make your product/company unique. If you cannot answer the above questions and list three things, you do not know what makes your company or product special. Either you do not have a niche or have not identified it. Go back to the beginning and start again. *Try to be more creative and have more fun, be daring and find your niche.* Then build it on a solid business foundation.

4. To Market To Market. You will need to get the word out. There are many ways to market today. Choose the best one for your project. Get testimonials from happy customers so others know you are real and that your system works. Get free advertising by writing press releases and sending them to every press contact you can think of. Explore direct marketing, television, radio, newspapers, trade publications, magazines, flyers, internet, mail, etc. Word of mouth is powerful. Offer incentives. Test in each market you find. When you find what works for you, repeat, do more testing and tweaking. Marketing is fun, a creative medium, and is always evolving!

5. Work your plan. Yes, this does mean you need to stop planning at some point and WALK BOLDLY — TAKE ACTION! This is where some get hung up. They know what they are supposed to be doing but just do not follow through. Once you are organized, you have found and proven your niche and believe strongly in your product or service, TAKE ACTION, *stick to it, repeat the process and stay determined until you reach success.*

6. Look back and learn.
   A. Repeat what works.
   B. Don't repeat what doesn't work.
   C. "Turn the rock" and look for special market niches that you can fill for the market, customers, lenders, etc.

www.mentorsmagazine.com

7. Look forward and learn. Invest in yourself, continue your education. Sometimes you hear something new and exciting; sometimes you hear a lot of what you already know; but if you listen very carefully, almost without fail you will find some little "jewel of wisdom" that will kick your business or business techniques up a notch.

8. Give back to the community. Use 10% of your profits and/or 10% of your time to make a difference in the lives of others and in your community. We believe in the universal truth of "what goes around comes around." Be thankful and appreciate what you have accomplished and have yet to accomplish. We believe that you should go through life with one hand up and one hand down. Whatever help you have had along the way — be it spiritual, financial, emotional or gifts of guidance — pass that gift along to others. Do not be the one to break that chain of helping others.

Casey & Byron Kellar manage a successful manufacturing company and have developed millions of dollars in real estate properties. Casey is a published writer, consultant, and speaker on business and success. More information is available at:
www.rainshadowlabs.com
ckcrent-ownhomes.com
TurnTheRock.com

What If The Navy SEALS Taught Real Estate?

Tactical Mentoring

by Todd Dotson

It was just past 5:00 AM on a cold winter morning. A handful of individuals and I quietly boarded the aircraft and settled in for a two hour flight. What should have been a routine flight was soon interrupted by turbulent weather and the pilot's voice over the intercom telling us to lock down for the remainder of the trip. The rough weather did little to interrupt the focus of my team and me, only depriving us of a little extra shuteye.

Not long after, the pilot was back on the intercom reporting that inclement weather had forced us to change the primary drop zone and land the plane at a secondary site. Once on the ground, my team quickly assembled and headed to the predetermined staging area rallying with the indigenous personnel.

We quickly headed over to our AO (Area of Operation) only to be slowed by icy conditions and rough roads. Slowed temporarily, we arrived at the target area and began conducting immediate operations.

It wasn't long before we identified multiple targets and moved to take down the primary target.

Needless to say it was another successful OP … .

What I've just described wasn't a SEAL team conducting military operations, but the Tactical Real Estate Team conducting property operations on behalf of our students. It's what I refer to as a property sweep and Rochester, NY was the target.

As the sun began to rise, we debriefed over breakfast. In all, we had identified just over a 100 targets, prioritized our takedown, and put the first five under contract — one target property was bought for a dollar and sold in "As Is" condition for $2,300.

"If the Navy SEALS taught real estate investing, there's no question they would be teaching Todd Dotson's Tactical System. I know because I was a Navy SEAL … ."
— Ty Valkanas, Real Estate Investor/Mentor, Former Navy SEAL

47

The following week we were in San Jose. Favorable weather conditions allowed for a smooth drop into the staging area. East San Jose was the first AO — you remember, Area of Operation. Multiple targets identified with two under contract. The first bought for $352,000.00 and sold in "As Is" condition for $375, 000.00. The second was a preforeclosure taken down "Subject To" and sold utilizing a short sale with the Lender.

Two weeks later we dropped into Orange County, California and quickly proceeded to Santa Ana and then to Long Beach. Next we headed to Phoenix and dropped into the "Presidents Streets" to target Ugly Houses and then reassembled in Scottsdale to work some Luxury Homes …

When this book is released, I'll be conducting operations in San Francisco and Oakland.

The outcome? It's always the same … When the Navy SEALS hit, they leave a body count. When Tactical Real Estate hits, we leave a property count.

I trust you've enjoyed the operational breakdown. It's funny — when we go out to mentor students they're always expecting us to bring the "Magic Bullet!" When our time together concludes, they realize they're the magic bullet. We just helped them strategically grid their market, successfully acquire the target, quickly line up the weapon of choice (wholesale, subject to, lease option, short sale, etc.) and tactically pull the trigger!!! You see it's not how much information you have that counts; it's the quality of the "Intel" that really matters. It's being able to evaluate, understand, and implement where you live — that's my expertise.

If what I've just described gets your juices flowing, then welcome to Tactical Real Estate™. If not, I'd prefer to know now. Not everybody makes the cut, and just because you have a Gold Card doesn't mean you qualify. Contrary to what many of the Gurus on the mass market tell you, not everybody is cut out to be a full-time investor. When we come to train you, the only easy day was yesterday. When we drop in, it's on.

Regardless of who provided your foundational training, Tactical Real Estate™ can help you implement where you live.

Listen, if you haven't replaced the income on your job and you want to, you can't afford not to have us drop in and conduct operations on your behalf. I've found over the years that those that have a strong burning desire to succeed and haven't turned the corner are precisely the ones that need Tactical Mentoring the most. People are smart if you'll just show them how. People don't mind paying for training as long as the training pays for itself. Is it any wonder I developed the slogan, "The Checks Don't Lie™." It's my call to the industry to produce results or make way for someone who can.

By now I'm sure I've piqued the curiosity of some and ruffled the feathers of others … … GOOD! I'm not here to win friends, just influence people. You can do it. More importantly, you deserve to be able to do it!

"Your no nonsense approach to training helped us build our business the right way. Today we are creating cash and building wealth as evidenced by the attached check of $149,492.91. The checks certainly don't lie!™"
> — Katy McKinney, Real Estate Investor/Mentor

While I'm thinking about it, be sure to check out my June 04 cover story in Mentors Magazine. Better yet, call my office at 1-800 RE DEALS and request the bound copy of my reality-based interview with Linda Forsythe. I don't think she would mind me saying that my command of the nation's real estate markets surprised even her!

5 Keys to Your Success

Sustained success in this business comes down to five key ingredients:
- Creating Inventory
- Successfully Tracking/Contacting Owners
- Quickly Determining Your Prospects
- Writing Simple, Reality Based Offers
- Having High-Speed Exit Strategies

"Thanks for finally taking us out of the audience!"
> — Roger M., Phoenix, Arizona

Since we just covered five keys to sustained success in this business, let me address three common misconceptions or myths about real estate investing.

Three Myths About Real Estate Investing

1. **MYTH** — Investing in real estate is a surefire road to financial independence. FACT — most real estate investors don't survive their first portfolio of properties …

2. **MYTH** — Real estate investing is all about Location, Location, Location. FACT — Location is important if you live there or you're holding for appreciation. Otherwise, it's all about the DEAL, the DEAL, the DEAL …

3. **MYTH** — If you buy it, they will come. FACT — you're not Kevin Costner, and this isn't the "Field of Dreams." Buy it right and they will come, buy it wrong and you're in trouble …

I hope you've enjoyed this article, but it's time to Fast Rope into the LZ (Landing Zone), and get after it. If you are just getting started and always had a strong desire to succeed in real estate, now is your chance. If you are starting over and a casualty of training that was long on promises and short on delivery, it's your chance to do it right. If you're already on the fast track and want to make sure you stay there, let us ensure your success.

What if the Navy SEALS taught Real Estate? They don't, but fortunately we do, and we are coming to a city near you. Understand, reality based training easily pays for itself. Without it, most are doomed for failure. If you are serious about real estate investing, you are going to pay for my Mentor Program one way or another. Going it alone may well cost you time, money, and quite possibly financial freedom. A former student, close friend, and current mentor on my team said it best.

"Todd, your training was life changing. As a West Point graduate and Army Ranger, I understand what it means to be reality based. As a member of the elite Army Rangers, we had a saying that, 'No one gets left behind.' Today I'm privileged to be part of another elite unit. At Tactical Real Estate, we have another saying, 'No student gets left behind.'"
— Lt. Colonel John Angell, U.S. Army Ranger Retired, Real Estate Investor/Mentor

My friend, don't get left behind in the wasteland of books, tapes, and generic real estate boot camps … Let us drop in and escort you to safety and financial security.

The Checks Don't Lie™

P.S.: Remember, real estate investing is not a Hobby and Hope is not a course of action. Get In, Get Out, and Get Paid!

Todd Dotson of Arlington, Texas is the founder of Tactical Real Estateĺ and the Nation's foremost authority on getting in, getting out, and getting paid. With an emphasis on "buying and selling" to create immediate cash and a system for parlaying that into wealth, he brings a reality based approach to the business of real estate investing. As the developer of the Country's first nation-wide on site mentoring program, Todd has the unique advantage of having mentored students in every major market in the Country — a claim that only he and his team can make! Hands-on experience allows him to seamlessly combine wholesale buying and purchase option strategies — Anywhere, USA.

Todd instructs his students to go "ugly often" and "pretty when it's profitable!" The results speak for themselves as does Todd's trademark slogan, "The Check's Don't Lie."

To learn more about Todd Dotson and Tactical Real Estate, visit his website at www.TacticalRealEstate.com

Systemize For Success in Your Real Estate Business:

10 Easy systems to double your current income or get you off to a successful start!

by Linda Lossick-Longstreet

"If you think you can, or if you think you can't, you are right." — Peter Fortunato

When I first started in the real estate business, I thought all there was to it was to just buy property, sell property, and make money. After several transactions, sloppy paperwork, no systems, (couldn't find anything), I soon discovered that without a good simple set of systems, I could not continue to run the business. Things were falling through the cracks; deals were lost because I didn't have a good follow-up system. I overlooked tax deductions and opened myself up to lawsuits. Worst of all, I lost income!

So I quickly started doing research and learning how to set up systems to run my real estate business correctly. I implemented my systems one by one, slowly redirecting my business. What an amazing change! Things started flowing more smoothly, and the deals started flowing in rapidly. More deals than I could handle! I knew it was time to hire an assistant. It was so exciting to finally get my buying and selling machine flowing with ease.

Michael Gerber draws the vital, often overlooked distinction between working *on* your business and working *in* your business. It is soooo important to use your time to work on your business, and use your Real Estate Wealth Team to work in your business. This frees you up to work on what you do best — Buy Houses!!!!

1. Your Roadmap to Financial Freedom

Think of the big picture! Before you set up another system, you must know where you are going. You need a road map. A step-by-step plan from your present situation to where you would like to be.

First, you must decide where you want to be in the future. What are you working toward? Where would you like to be in 10 years? Would you like to have a second home at the beach? $20,000 per month passive income? Travel the world? Whatever it is for you, write it down.

51

Next you will need to decide where you want to be in five years. How far toward your 10-year goal would you like to be? $10,000 per month in passive income? $1 million in assets? Thirty rental properties? Write it all down and make it real. Make a plan. Now three years. Break it down some more.

Now plan next year. Where would you like to see yourself by the end of next year? Make it very clear and concise, so you can picture it. What systems will you have in place? How many rentals will you have? How many houses will you buy and rehab? How many will you wholesale? How much each month? Would you like to have a wholesaling machine?

Now finish out this year. Make a plan. What systems will you have in place? By what month? How much advertising will you do? How many houses will you buy? How many will you keep? How many do you need to keep each month to reach your 10-year goal?

Take these goals you have created from now to 10 years and make your self a roadmap to success! Map it out, step by step! These are your dreams mapped out, just the way you want them.

2. The Ultimate Office Organizer

Have you ever needed a document for closing and you couldn't find it or even find the file you thought it should be in? Think of how much extra time you spent looking for things in your office. Just think of how much time you could be spending instead finding more deals! What if you had a system where you could find anything in your office in minutes? Wouldn't that would make your life so much easier?

I now have a simple system like that and it saves me many hours per week. You can too! Just set your office up using a numbering system, where all you have to do is look at a list in the front of each file drawer to know where everything is in your office. You will start numbering your files instead of putting names on them. It is a simple to use program that comes with software to guide you through the process. When you type in a key word, the program will tell you where to look. So simple, anyone can use it! You can get it at www.wealthatoz.com

Have you ever wished you could just have someone else take all your phone calls? I did for a long time. Then I got smart and started using a system that pre-screened all my calls. It leads them to separate mail boxes that give the callers the general information they need. Then when they call me, they have already been pre-screened. All from a simple phone line in your office! You can set up the entire system yourself. Once you have the system set up, there are no further costs to you, except your monthly local phone bill. You can even choose to use a toll-free number if you'd like.

With all this extra time, you are going to be able to buy more houses than you ever could have imagined!!!! The income of your dreams is just around the corner.

3. Marketing Made Simple

Marketing to buy houses — With a well thought-out and well-established buying machine, you will be able to find as many deals as you can handle. You will never wonder where your next deal is coming from! (Or your next paycheck!) You will know each week exactly what step you will take in your plan, and what you will need to do to keep the phone ringing and the deals coming. You will also know where you stand in relationship to your marketing budget, how much your leads are costing you, and when to add to your marketing plan.

Marketing to sell houses — By setting up and following a simple four-step selling program, you will get into action, and out of reaction! Your plan will guide you to make the next decision in your selling plan without having to re-think your plan each time. It is already in place — a no-brainer! Your property will be sold before you know it!

4. The Deal Funder

Ron LeGrand says, "When you find the deals, the money will find you." This is so true! I have never had a hard time funding a good deal. There are many places you can look for private funds. Ask all the professionals and non-professionals you know: other investors, mortgage brokers, realtors, attorneys, doctors, dentists, hairdressers, barbers, anyone you can think of. Everyone likes a good deal. And no credit check!

You can also check with local banks. If you have decent credit, local banks are a good source of funding your rehabs for a low interest rate. It is easy to develop a good rapport with your local banker. They will also be willing to loan to you in your business name, so it does not show up on your personal credit report.

5. The Team Builder

What is more important than building your real estate wealth team? Who can help you achieve your goals? Who has the skills and the expertise? Who will assist you to move to the next level?

Here are some of the people you may want to consider on your real estate wealth team: real estate attorney, tax attorney, accountant, bookkeeper, assistant, sales-person, contractor, handyman, property manager, banker, private lenders, unskilled labor, and anyone else you can think of that will help you to accomplish your goals. You must also consider a good time to add these people to your team. What qualities should they possess? What values should they have? Are you ready for them? How much should you pay? How will you find them? How will you screen them?

6. The People Problem Solver

Real estate is a people business before it is an asset, or a real estate business. You are in the business of solving people's problems, so you might as well get used to it. Once you know what the problem is, you can get to work on solving it, and making the deal happen. To close the deal, like Stephen Covey says, "You must create a win/win situation."

In business and personal life, it is imperative to be honest and "in integrity" at all times. If you slip, correct it. This is your best defense, and your best offense. As Gay Hendricks says, "Do what you say you will do, and don't do what you say you won't do." This will cut down immensely on the conflict in your life and your business life! This can also be a way to cut down on angry customers who could sue you otherwise. Stick with your word, or make a new agreement with the other party. Don't change the terms without getting the other party to agree.

7. The Money Management Tool *(Or the Chunka Theory?)*

There were times in my business, as I am sure there were times in yours, when you did business by the chunka theory. A chunka money in and a chunka money out. No real rhyme or reason to it — never really knowing what each property was making, or losing. You find out later when your accountant puts it all together and tells you how much you lost or made on a deal. Tax time is a real eye opener.

You can set up a simple accounting system to help you keep track of all your purchases, expenses, and profits on your deals. You can turn it in to your accountant quarterly, or as frequently as you like, and know where your financial plan is going.

What a freeing feeling that is to know where you are financially from week to week! Know where you are, and where you are going!

8. The Safety Net

Step-by-Step Asset Protection

You are working hard to build your business and your assets for retirement. Do you want to make it easy for anyone to take them away? Of course not! You will protect them using whatever means you know.

It is time to decide what kind of business structure you want. You now have a few deals under your belt and know this is the business you want to be in. You have your 10-year plan, and know what you will need to protect. Do you need a C-Corporation, an S-Corporation, an LLC, an FLP, an LP, or do you want to put everything in your own personal name so anyone can find it if they tried?

It is time to find out the pros and cons of each and make some decisions that will fit your plan. Then you can have your attorney assist you to set up your business and your asset plan the way you choose.

9. Property Management Made Simple

A great property management/tenant management system is critical! It can make a huge financial difference and make your life much simpler! If you have an efficient property management system, you can trust the projections on your rents. If not, it will be haphazard to say the least. If you fill your properties with, "not so good tenants," you are asking for a roller coaster ride of property management. Learn to manage your tenants, so they are not managing you!!!!!!!

10. The Mistake Eliminator

Due diligence will save you a lot of mistakes, money, and headaches in the long run in your real estate business. Know what you are buying, from whom, and exactly what terms you agreed on. Use your team of real estate wealth professionals whenever you are in doubt of your qualifications to make a judgment in a deal. Some professionals to consider are: inspectors, appraisers, structural engineers, surveyors, pest control specialists, attorneys, accountants, and other real estate investors. *Now Take Action!!!!!!!!!!!!!!!!!!!!!!!!!!!!!!!!!*

As you can see, systemizing your real estate business is the important next step to launch you into the future you have been dreaming of!

Linda Lossick-Longstreet is a full time Real Estate investor with over 15 years of real estate experience. She specializes in retail, wholesale and rental real estate as well as teaching and mentoring others on how to get started and/or how to improve their existing real estate business.

For detailed information on systemizing your real estate business and maximizing your profits for success or to order your FREE SPECIAL REPORT: HOW TO SYSTEMIZE YOUR REAL ESTATE BUSINESS FOR SUCCESS, *go to www.wealthatoz.com, or call Linda Lossick-Longstreet at 912-898-2112, or write me at LLL@wealthatoz.com*

Harvard
on the
Highway of Life

by Phillip Warrick

As a beginning real estate investor at the young age of 24, I am honored to share my story with you. It is my hope that it may somehow inspire and encourage you in any venture you may choose.

Background

I was born in 1980 in Pasadena, TX. In 1981 my parents felt called to Brazil as missionaries, and it was there that I spent the first ten years of my life. My parents were very proud to establish and build many churches that are still in operation today. Growing up, I spent a lot of time in church and accepted Christ as my savior around the age of 7. Coming from a religious family has shaped who I am today.

As a kid, I traded my American dollars to make a little extra money. The American dollar is always worth more in Brazil, and I usually had several from gifts and visitors. Brazilians used to call me a little Jew because I was so good with money. When I was ten, the schools in Brazil went on strike. My parents made the decision to send me, my sister, and my brother back to the U.S.A. to continue our schooling. After about three months, they felt the best decision for our family was to move back indefinitely.

Shortly after our return to Texas, my father decided to go into business for himself. He started a sign company called RS Graphics, and it proved to be a great success. I have always been very interested in business. At the age of 13, I would gladly opt out of playing with friends after school to instead go to work for my dad. It was there I was able to experience first hand business, finance, real life, and how to make it. I not only had the opportunity, but also the desire to watch my father work hard and reap the benefits of being self-employed. This gave me an entrepreneurial mindset.

During junior high, I started my first business selling bubble gum to my classmates for 25 cents apiece. I was making a great profit, considering I only paid $10–$15 at Sam's Wholesale for a 450 piece bucket! You do the math — not bad for a 13-year-old!

Toward the end of my senior year, I started thinking about the possibility of making money with real estate. My goal was to purchase a home and lease out the rooms to college students. I bought books on real estate and studied. During that same year, I was introduced to Lindsey Schultz, and it wasn't long before we became pretty serious. After graduation, Lindsey's mother talked her into going away to college. I don't know if she did this to get Lindsey away from me, or if she truly wanted her to experience college life on her own, but it didn't work. I packed my things and followed her. I moved into an apartment, went to college part time, and began working at a local sign company. After one semester, Lindsey and I started moving in different directions. We decided to split ways. I moved home, but continued paying for the apartment until the lease was up so it wouldn't damage my credit.

Back home I decided to work for a bank and not surprisingly, loved every minute of it. I was in my element, dressing in a shirt and tie and going to work to count money. After six months, I realized I didn't want to spend the rest of my life climbing the corporate ladder and find at the age of 65 that I was too tired from climbing to enjoy my retired years. I wanted to own the corporate ladder! I just didn't know how.

A New Life

I put in my two weeks notice and went back to college to figure out what I wanted to do with my life. It didn't take long to realize that school was not for me. I dropped my classes and decided to move to Colorado to live out my dream of snowboarding. My friend Todd and I moved together and found jobs as housemen at a local resort hotel with employee housing.

One week after starting my new job, I received a shocking, life changing phone call. My father was in the hospital, diagnosed with pancreatic cancer. Within 24 hours, I was back in Texas. My father had only months to live. He went to be with the Lord on April 5, 2000 at the age of 44. I guess God takes the best when He is ready — not when we are. After my father passed away, my mother and I worked to keep RS Graphics alive.

In 2001, Lindsey and I made our way back together. We were soon married and became parents to our first daughter, Raylea. We decided to live with my mother instead of throwing money away on rent, until we could save enough to purchase a home. It wasn't long. By February of 2002 we became first time homeowners. Soon we realized living with my mother and working with her every day had become a big burden on her. She was not recovering very well from our father's death. My sister, brother and I convinced her to move to Florida where she would be close to her sister and mother. It was time for a new beginning for her.

Once she decided to sell her home and make preparations to move to Florida, Lindsey and I saw the opportunity to purchase her house with the intention of

57

keeping it as a rental property. I had recently gone on a real estate cruise — a vacation with an education — and was pumped to get some rental properties. While there I was introduced to a book called *Rich Dad, Poor Dad* by Robert Kiyosaki. I was ready to put my newfound knowledge to work. We began paperwork with our mortgage broker, who misunderstood our investment intention. We were approved for 100% financing, but the loan stipulated that we must live in the house. We decided to rent our first house to a family who could not use a bank for financing due to a divorce and bad credit.

Research and Reading

After much research and reading, I was convinced that the best deal for both parties would be a 3-year lease with the option to buy the house. Part of the monthly rent payment was applied to the purchase price, so when they chose to purchase the house, we considered the rent credits as part of their down payment. This is often referred to as a rent-to-own. The couple that moved in liked the deal because they had some credit issues and were self-employed, making it hard to prove income to qualify for a loan. This way they had a few years to clean up their credit and establish their new company.

Just after moving into our second home, we were blessed with our second daughter, ReAnna. Our next income property came to us in June of 2003. We were able to negotiate a lease with the option to purchase a beautiful, 3-bedroom, 2-bath, 2-car garage house on a golf course. The home had been totally remodeled two years prior and was in perfect condition in a prime location, situated on a cul-de-sac. The seller had recently re-married and already moved out of the house. We rented the house to a couple on an 18-month lease. Unfortunately, these tenants never paid their rent on time. After about 11 months they moved out with no warning, without paying the last month's rent. This time, we sold it as a rent to own, as we will do from now on. This allows us to get more money up front as a down payment, and the tenants have an owner's mindset, making them more inclined to take care of *their* home.

In November of 2003, Todd gave me a lead that one of his friends was losing his house to foreclosure. He had fallen six months behind on his payments and already moved out of the house, counting it as a loss. After some minor repairs, the house gave us 20% or more in equity. We were able to stop the foreclosure by paying the six back payments. We took over his existing financing, painted the house, put new carpet in and sold it as a rent to own. A very nice couple lives in the house, takes great care of it and pay on time. They recently filed bankruptcy and were told by a realtor they could not even get into an apartment with their damaged credit. They thought they were going to be homeless until they found us. We love to help people in these kinds of situations because we know we're doing a good deed.

After this deal, I became very interested in investing full time. We were very excited to make a better living doing what we enjoy, helping people, having more freedom, and spending more time with our family. We owner-financed RS Graphics and held on to the property as a rental to the new owner. This lease, our fourth investment property, gave us the ability to be full-time real estate investors from our home.

In February 2004, we picked up another house from a divorcing couple. We gave them some moving money and they owner-financed their house to us. Any time we find a seller willing to finance all or part of the mortgage, we can usually structure a good deal. We got a tenant buyer in the house who moved out after two months with no warning. They left the house a mess, in need of new carpet and paint, and the back yard infested with fleas — but they had given a big enough down payment to get the house back to normal. This contract, like every other contract, has been a learning experience in how to choose the best tenant buyer.

A Valuable Roadtrip

In June of 2004 my family and I set out on a one-month road trip. The trip included a three-day seminar in Atlanta on neuro linguistic programming (NLP) with foreclosure expert Bill Twyford. The principles he teaches are great for anyone considering working in the foreclosure part of this business. Combine his teachings with that of Jeff Kaller, also known as www.mrpreforeclosure.com, and you'll have a powerful advantage over your competition.

From Atlanta, we visited my grandmother in Tennessee, and then Lindsey's grandparents in Wisconsin. While in WI we took the girls to The Mall of America, and on our way out I noticed a Barnes and Noble and could not resist buying Donald Trump's new book, *How to Get Rich*. The book is so good I read it in one sitting, and I would recommend everyone read it. We then headed to Orlando, Florida to attend a seminar held by Ron LeGrand. I bought all of Ron LeGrand's materials, which has proven to be the best move I've made in my real estate investing career. His courses have put everything into perspective and helped me to organize my business better.

On the 16-hour drive home, we listened to Ron's CD's. The one-month trip included over 4800 miles of listening to different courses and motivational materials, which I refer to as "Harvard on the Highway." The first two weeks after returning home, we spent some time putting out signs and different marketing materials. I was able to set up a nice at-home office, and on the third week the phone started ringing. I ended up putting three deals together in that one week.

One is the best deal we've made yet. On Wednesday, three days after sending out letters to people whose loans were in default, a lady called asking if we could buy her house. They had fallen behind 12 months on their mortgage and the house was scheduled for foreclosure on the following Tuesday. On Thursday I took all the necessary paperwork and a sales contract to her and got everything signed. I opened title on the house on Friday. The title company faxed the contract to the mortgage company, who agreed to stop the foreclosure process. Our next step will be to borrow money to buy, hold, and fix up the property, then re-sell it at market value.

As you can see, we are really exited about our new business. Growing up, I was taught to give 10% of my income to God, known as tithing. Now that I'll be making more money, I am excited to know my tithes will have a greater impact. I have a vision of helping churches apply the investment strategies I'm implementing in my personal life. I want to help at least one church per year become financially free. I will start a management company to manage investments for churches and the portfolios of other real estate investors. We have great plans for the future, and we know who holds the future. God has a work in progress through my family and me.

From trading dollars and selling bubble gum as a child, I have now moved to purchasing real estate in my early twenties to earn a living. I'm not sure what God has for my future, but I am sure that without Him nothing in my life would be possible. I'm on my knees every day giving God thanks and knowing He has greater things yet to come. Stay focused on Him and your burning desires and you can accomplish anything!

Contact Phillip Warrick at pwarrick@houston.rr.com
www.flippinhouses.com
www.makethemovenow.com

Which is right for you?

Mentoring, Teaching, Tutoring, Coaching

by Larry Grimaldi

I was sitting in a boot camp/event with my friend Steve Freeman and nearly 2000 other Real Estate Investors in Orlando, Florida. We both had already gotten our credit cards out and were in possession of our new box of "goodies" to make us great investors!

I turned to Steve and said, "What do you want from this event?"

"I need a Mentor!" he replied. I blinked.

"Steve, you've been in Real Estate investing for two years now. You just closed one deal where you bought 104 houses last week."

"Yep, I want a Mentor."

Mentoring, the Start

Our first great mentor — was Mom/Dad if we were lucky! (S)he:
- shaped our thinking
- gave us values
- opened up our visions
- painted our dreams
- trained us to do and act
- expanded our skills
- celebrated our successes and achievements
- hung in through our failures
- was our friend and confidant
- was always there just to talk to

Many mothers/fathers achieved these things with little education, few skills, poor economic privilege, small financial means and limited social/family support. Parents share this early mentoring position with grandparents, aunts, uncles and others depending upon the family structure.

61

Some children go through these early years with incredible negative pressures and surroundings. People like this would confound Freud and friends because, in spite of their difficult upbringing, many of them reach incredible levels of success and become role models for others.

Enter "THE THING" — School

Formal Education has arrived. It fills up years of our lives, stresses even parents out, and will soak up whole days at a gulp.

Can you remember the name of your first teacher? Of course! I never met someone who can't! These teachers most often are under paid and under appreciated. They have a "calling" for the lack of an extensive explanation for their profession. They made school fun; learning was exciting and rewarding! The whole world came alive. (OK, the times tables Dad drilled us every morning on the way to school was tedious! But I'll never forget!)

Teachers teach. Knowledge of teacher passes to student who now possesses the knowledge. This is the premise of schooling. However, some teachers cross the line! Not content with merely passing facts and knowledge, they:

- Inspire
- Motivate
- Stimulate
- Awaken genius and create future aspiration

A simple "You are college material" from a respected teacher turns a statement into an expectation and a goal. Standard group educational learning achievement levels do not guarantee student achievement. Often more is needed.

America's education system is based on class/group not the individual. But the individuals are not without hope. Hope and help are galloping towards them with hands out.

Tutoring is the Hired Gun

It is private. It is personal. It is paid for.
- Trouble in math class?
- Can't seem to write a term paper?
- Fat and flabby?
- Back swing need help?
- Weak foreclosure buying skill?
- Computer illiterate?
- Marketing results stink?
- Marriage in trouble?

Tutoring comes with many names attached, such as personal trainer, consultant, instructor, advisor, counselor.

Tutoring presupposes a simple fact: **you** need to know your problem/need before **you** hire this professional. The current fashion is to present testimonies. The bigger the better. If a check for $100,000 is good, just think about one for $800,000!

Hire me, buy my books, go to my boot camp! This is very effective and powerful. (Ask me how I know this! Or look at my bookcase!)

Some are selling "tutoring" to the masses. Short-term packages of personal counseling by company-trained reps, cookie-cutter counseling on your chosen subject. This person is your hired friend — you give him cash! Don't need a friend? OK, maybe this next person is just what you need!!!

Coaching

"The coach" is generally a sports term. Yes, I understand "mothers-to-be" have hi-jacked this term in the Lamaze program. I also submit that I have not heard the term "coach" stick around long after birth!

The coach is a person who imparts knowledge, hones abilities, sharpens skills, motivates, cultivates focus and develops a winning attitude. The coach is paid to produce a winner, not to be a pal.

Be it chess or baseball, the repeatable practice of the skill or action combined with the strategy of a winning plan as given by the coach results in a desired goal. The coach's mandate/job depends on his ability to mold others into his system. This system is his way to be a winner.

Interestingly, there is a huge difference in style/methods to achieve the "winning" goals. Walt Disney Pictures produced the movie "Miracle," the true story of the 1980 United States Ice Hockey team's triumphant Olympic victory over the Soviet Union. It is a classic story of a coach who changes his methods to achieve a goal. Methods used are often not pleasant or kindly! Rude, harsh, demanding — in your face yelling and screaming, total disregard for feelings or sensitivities is not unheard of! It is not human nature to live or function outside our present comfort zone. This a coach knows. He also knows that we are capable of achieving levels of success that we normally only dream of achieving.

My personal high school coach was the ultimate athlete, a Hawaiian, great in every sport who confirmed his abilities and skills on the field of play. He reminded me of my favorite wild-west hero, Wyatt Earp, who entered every shooting contest and always won! Intimidation does work!

The original geniuses I call the "Mozarts." They are the few who do the creating the first time. The "genius performers" are the Einsteins who take theory through the portal to reality.

These geniuses take reality/data, analyze it, organize it, distill it and then present their insights that change business, organizations and lives. We stand in awe of their achievements even thought they are so simple that we say, "I knew that. I just never saw it like that!" Or my favorite, "Why didn't I think of that or see it?"

To name just a few of these geniuses:
- Napolean Hill
- Jim Callen
- Albert Leroy
- Robert Allen
- Robert Kiyosaki
- Ron LeGrand

Sometimes, however, I encounter a common problem, one that I share with many others. Standing on the shoulders of these great geniuses, I tend to forget the basics — even such simple concepts as asset/liability, good debt/bad debt, focus and goals. From time to time, revisiting these geniuses' work, I am reminded that they have given us their knowledge and insights in a usable clear map for our success.

Books and stories of success and greatness abound; our curiosity, our desire to know "how did they do it" drives us to read. Unspoken, however, is "Can I copy them, can I do it, can I be great like them?"

On our journey to this level of genius — we want help. We need help! We need a Mentor!

True Mentors will have some of these universal distinguishing characteristics:

1. Possesses a skill level you want, often outside your comfort zone
2. Has done what you want to do successfully
3. Unlike teachers, tutors and coaches, most often is NOT paid
4. Relationships often lasts years, but not always
5. Requires a good deal of time (which holds most back from being mentors)
6. Do not want to waste time and effort on the uncommitted/not driven
7. Willing to share the whole life experience — very personal

Now it stands to reason the next question should be "OK, so how do I find my true mentor?" Friend or acquaintance, paid or not, summer or winter, the answer remains simply — **ASK … ASK** for help, **ASK** for direction, **ASK** for ideas. **ASK**. The second and bigger answer is like the first — **ASK** — but be prepared to give back/exchange for your mentoring. Are you willing to:

1. Give time — "work in their office for free"
2. Be a personal assistant. (read "go-for" — or slave!)
3. "May I take you to dinner?"
4. "May I spend a day with you?"
5. Think creative here

Remember:
- Education from teaching is never ending and our basic foundation.
- Tutoring keeps our skills on the progressive edge.
- Coaching sharpens what we are outside our comfort zone.

True Mentoring has some of the elements of each but is more like adoption! A mentor takes the personal interest, invests the time and — like it or not — like family, will give us the kick in the pants we need!

Be prepared to step up to the challenges a mentor will set before you. Ask yourself "What am **I** willing to commit to achieve this mentoring?" Now ring the bell. If there is only one thought you take away, it should be this: **be persistent and relentless** toward this mission of mentor finding. Ring the bell again. Your success will depend on this.

… to find a true mentor is rare and wonderful …
… by far the most rewarding …
… So go for it!

Contact Larry Grimaldi
1600 E. Florida
Hemet CA 92544
Phone: 909-658-725
www.we-sell-lgrimaldi.successfast.net/

Is Real Estate an Investment or a Business?

by Loral Langemeier

Many individuals that I coach/mentor come to me with the perception that real estate is the answer to all their wealth building problems. In fact, most come to us wanting to make $5K/month in passive income through real estate.

I want to tell you that it is absolutely possible to create $5,000/month in passive income. Furthermore, it is absolutely possible to create tens of thousands dollars per month in passive income, as well as to create a net worth of millions of dollars.

However, what people don't realize is that to generate $5K/month in passive income, you must treat real estate as a business first and an investment second. When you take the time to create a sophisticated real estate business, it will then become your most valuable investment asset.

So, what does it take to set up and run a real estate business?

I am going to take you through 6 steps that you must use to build YOUR Real Estate business.

These steps are:

- Vision
- Strategy/Tactics
- Revenue Modeling
- Entity Structuring and Tax Strategies
- Remarketing/Sales
- Leadership of your Real Estate Wealth Team

Vision

It is important to design your vision for real estate to determine your focus and strategy. It is critical to determine this early in your real estate career.

Your vision should contain three parts:

- Purpose
- Missions
- Values

Purpose is the ultimate intention of your business. It is the "why your company exists" statement.

The mission of a company is comprised of the big initiatives you are going to accomplish. It is composed of goals and activities that you could check off when completed; it is not a destination.

The values of your company speak to your true essence and represent who you are and what you stand for. Keep in mind that experts agree that if a person were to lose one of their core values they would be a completely different person. Others claim that we die for our values before we compromise them.

Strategy & Tactics

As you think about how you want to acquire properties, you have to determine your area of focus. Think about the different types of real estate and the different results that they will create for you. These are things such as residential real estate, raw land development, industrial/commercial real estate, multi-unit/multi-tenant buildings, and retail space. This can also include rehabs, flips, HUD, VA, and lease options.

As you can see from the above descriptions, there are multiple options available to acquire properties. Again, as you look at what your strategy will be for property acquisition, it's most important that you get focused on a very small niche, learn that business of real estate and do it very well. Over time, as you're more sophisticated, you'll begin to take on larger projects with a variety of investors and Field Partners. But to get started — focus.

Revenue Modeling

Revenue modeling has two components:

- The determination of a base line (where your business is financially).
- Forecasting projected revenue (tied specifically to your strategies).

Revenue drives your business and will decide your future results! As harsh as that may seem, it's the absolute bottom line. The purpose of business is to make a profit and if you're not doing that, you're not running a business.

Entity Structuring

Protecting your wealth and your real estate assets is very important. This is done through proper entity structuring. We are very aggressive in working with real estate businesses and investors about this conversation of entity structuring. What most people don't understand is that real estate, unlike other assets, has a higher degree of liability because you typically have another person involved (i.e. renting from you, leasing from you, etc.). If something happened to this person on your property, they could sue you, which puts all of your other assets as risk.

Entity structuring provides the following:

- Asset Protection
- Protection from Unnecessary Liabilities
- The Use of Privacy for Protection
- Maximizing Tax Strategies

The goal of proper asset protection is to minimize your risk and to grow and sustain the asset base for generations. Our goal is that you have sustainable wealth.

Remarketing and Sales System

As you acquire your properties and rehab them, you need to be remarketing for tenant prospects as you go into the contract. How do you market the property for a rental, a lease or a sale? Whether you're marketing for a residential or commercial property, many of the following techniques will apply. Some techniques will be more useful in residential real estate and some techniques you'll need to tailor to commercial real estate ... but the bottom line is to get your word out.

There are several options for you to develop your remarketing system. Here are just a few:

- Advertise in the newspaper
- Fliers
- Radio
- Yard signage
- Word of mouth
- Mortgage brokers
- Realtors
- Check Cashing Stores
- Divorce and bankruptcy attorneys
- Credit repair classes
- First time homebuyer classes

Leadership of Your Real Estate Wealth Team

The last component of your acquisition system is your real estate wealth team. It can be a very critical component of property acquisition and should be taken very seriously. In fact, it can either make or break your deal. We've been talking about your acquisition team — people on your acquisition team will include your real estate agent/broker, inspectors, CPA, attorney, title company, your mortgage lender and more. In fact, we're dedicating a whole chapter to this topic later in the program. Real estate requires good leadership and communication skills to make sure your real estate program is done properly.

I trust if you are reading this book, you are at a crossroads in your life, and looking for your next steps. I have just laid out for you step by step how I transformed myself into a millionaire by the time I was thirty-four. I diligently worked on and through my financial conditioning. I clearly established my financial foundation. To this day I actively lead my wealth team to accelerate my wealth. Whether you are fourteen, forty-four or ninety four, the same is possible for you.

I highly encourage you to start these steps today. Don't hesitate any longer. Seize your success … choose your destiny … LIVE OUT LOUD.

To Your Wealth,
Loral Langemeier
© 2003 REV. 2004, Live Out Loud, Inc.

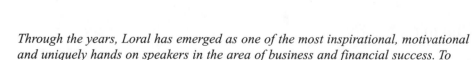

Through the years, Loral has emerged as one of the most inspirational, motivational and uniquely hands on speakers in the area of business and financial success. To find out how Loral can change your life, contact us at 888-262-2402, info@liveoutloud.com or www.liveoutloud.com

Navigating the Hurdles to Success

by Krystal Migliore

I spent the first thirty something years of my life following what I thought were the traditional rules for success:

- Get a good education
- Get a good job
- Work hard
- Get ahead

Then, one Friday afternoon, my boss told me that I didn't need to come in Monday. I assured him I didn't need another day off. I had just spent a year implementing a special project involving a major computer conversion to a new accounting and information system. Being a good employee, I had put my life on hold for a year and worked tons of extra hours. I had comp time accrued that I had gradually been using. My boss repeated that I didn't need to come in Monday. It took me a while to catch on that he wasn't trying to tell me to take time off; he was telling me not to come back. He finally told me that the company was laying off seven people, and I was one of them.

Looking back, I almost feel sorry for him. I don't think he had any experience laying someone off, and I was being exceptionally dense about the whole thing. But look at it from my viewpoint. I had never been ever been laid off before. After all, they had just given me a promotion and a sizeable raise. While I knew the company was having cash-flow problems, I was blindsided. I had just been thrown way out of my comfort zone. I felt like someone had cheated and it hadn't been me. I had followed the rules for success and someone hadn't played fair. Now I had two choices: I could blame the world for this tragic misfortune, or I could get on with my life.

Changing the Rules

After the shock wore off, I was determined to have more control over my destiny. If I were ever in this position again, it would be my fault — not due to someone else's inability to take care of business. I realized that I needed to make a few modifications to my rules for success.

The very next day, I fired up my entrepreneurial spirit. I used my contacts to establish myself as a business consultant working with small to mid-size publishers. I used my skills and the knowledge gained during that year-long special project to assist publishers in implementing the same specialty accounting and information systems.

Consulting was a great experience. I met wonderful people, did challenging and worthwhile work and was paid very well. The downside was that I was away from home way too much. My clients were scattered all over the United States. When I was home, I was exhausted. The biggest challenge was, "I had no control." Once I made a commitment to a client, I was on the hook until the assignment was completed.

One night when actually home, I saw a late night commercial. Yes, you guessed it. Real Estate. I decided if others had created wealth investing in real estate, there was no reason that I couldn't. So I decided to work into it slowly since I basically knew nothing about real estate. My husband Lee and I had bought and later sold our first residence, but we had used very traditional methods. We had a realtor show us properties until we found what we wanted. We went to a bank and got a loan. We moved in. When selling, we just followed the same formula. I had a lot to learn, plus I was still consulting.

After five years of consulting, I accepted a five-day job in Tennessee. Before I arrived, my new clients told me the system "wasn't working quite right." What was found when I arrived on site was a disaster. They had implemented their own conversion and then used the new system for ten months. The five-day job turned into four months while I started from scratch and created an entirely new database.

Talk about no control! This had happened before, but each time I had attributed it to a freak occurrence, something never to be repeated. Again, I had followed the rules but it hadn't worked quite like I expected. Finally I had to admit that, while I worked for myself, I had no control over my hours. It was just as bad — or worse — than being an employee. Plus, I really had no life. The time had come when something had to change. At this point probably more than a few of you can identify with my position. Have you been there and done that, too?

Changing the Definition

When I followed the traditional rules of success, it never occurred to me to question what defines "success." I vowed that I would now use a formula for success that was created by someone who actually had money and what I wanted even more … freedom.

71

Getting the education in real estate is essential — and the easiest part. The "how to" information is presented in detailed, easy-to-understand formats. Aren't we lucky there are so many people who have gone before us and are willing to share their experience and knowledge? Information on all facets of real estate investing is readily available and the pool of information is deep and ever growing.

I began devouring anything and everything that I could get my hands on that would tell me "how to" become successful as a real estate entreprenure. I wanted to buy houses. I turned my office and car into my classrooms. I attended live "hands on" conferences. Implementing the plan seemed easy because I just followed the instructions.

After following the real estate home buying plan a couple of times, I began to see a pattern. I had success, but something was holding me back. There were hurdles impeding my progress.

I remember when I ran hurdles on the high school track team, the hurdles were easy to identify. They looked the same and they were precisely the same height. There were exactly the same number of hurdles in each race and they were positioned in the same place every time. Each race, I knew exactly what to expect. I could practice the footwork required to clear the hurdles with ease, without stumbling or slowing down.

The hurdles I faced now weren't the same at all. I didn't know when and where they would pop up. I didn't know how many there would be. I didn't even know what the hurdles would look like. I really had no idea if I would slow down, stumble or even fall.

I'd like to share with you how I came to eventually recognize the hurdles I faced and how you can avoid them. The most important lesson I learned was to ask myself what was preventing me from taking the steps necessary to accomplish what I wanted to accomplish. What was stalling me? Why wasn't I forging ahead like other people who started at the same time I did? The answer turned out to be that I was the problem. I was responsible. Now that I had discovered the problem, I had to discover what I was doing or not doing that was impeding my progress.

Getting Started

The first realization was that I knew exactly what I needed to do, but I was putting off taking the steps I knew were required. I was getting ready, but really I was procrastinating. All of the materials mentioned it, but I still didn't recognize it. I now know that procrastination is actually due to a desire for perfection while I was waiting to get it perfect, everyone else was passing me by. They were moving and I wasn't.

Ask yourself, why not start now and do what is necessary? Don't wait for some magical, mystical starting point or for all of the planets to align, creating a perfect moment. Realize that there never will be a perfect moment. There is only now. Any other moment is in the past or the future. Nothing will ever be perfect. Everything will only be ready when you really need it. You might not know it all. But don't ever doubt your ability to learn what you need to know when you need it. What if the result is something less that the desired optimal result? Learn how to fix it.

Ask yourself … What if there was no "what if?"

Following the Right Rules

Secondly, I realized I wasn't following the recipe in the educational materials *exactly*. Even though I didn't know much about real estate or marketing, somehow I thought that I must know better. Let me put it this way … Picture yourself locked away in a vault filled with more money than you ever imagined. The amount is not important because it is all that you will ever need to do whatever you want. Freedom will be yours for the rest of your life. You will have the ability to touch and change as many lives as you choose for the rest of time.

Now, there is a time lock on the vault door. When that time lock is activated, the vault door will open and you will freely walk out into the sunshine, with your life, your health, your wealth and all of the advantages it will bring. Now picture a bomb sitting on the table in front of you, also locked in this vault. The timer on the bomb has been activated and is set to detonate just one minute *before* the time lock opens the vault door. Do you see a hurdle?

Sitting next to the bomb is the book *Instructions to Defuse this Bomb*. You have what I think would be an easy choice to make. You need to disarm the bomb. Are you going to use the instruction book? Don't you think it would be a good idea to follow the instructions step by step? Will you skip steps? Will you decide that you must know better than the expert who wrote the instructions? How many bombs have you defused lately?

If you don't follow the instructions exactly, how can you possibly expect the same successful results? In this case the results will be very measurable: the bomb explodes or it doesn't. If you have instructions that have been tested and perfected and achieved the desired results, wouldn't the best choice be to just follow them?

While the bomb never exploded in my face, I now understand how much faster I could have achieved success, if I just followed the directions from the experts! What will you do?

www.mentorsmagazine.com

Making It Win-Win for Everyone

At an early age, I had learned not to judge others; however, when working with prospective buyers or sellers, I found myself anticipating what others would do. I was projecting my values and past experiences onto them and I thought I knew what their answer would be even before I asked the question. I convinced myself that I knew the answer, so there was no reason to ask the question. I talked myself out of taking action on so many things that would have made a huge difference in the results.

It is never a good idea to judge others. Why people do what they do does not matter. It does not matter how they ended up where they are. What does matter is their motivation. What will solve their problem? Solving their problem and creating a win-win situation is the *only* thing that matters. When I am able to do that, the possibilities are unlimited.

Another invisible hurdle I discovered was the flip side of judging others. I was concerned about others judging me. I grew up to be very quiet and reserved in public. After about two years in the house buying business, I finally realized that I had been doing business as a stealth fighter. Every once in awhile, I made a hit, but most of the time, no one actually knew I was out there. I was keeping a low profile because I didn't want to call attention to myself for fear that someone might try to judge my motives. Learn to believe in yourself! Remember the old adage: "Fake it until you make it."

When I am able to create a win-win situation, I know that I have succeeded. I decided that I really don't care what someone else will think. I decided to make a few changes in the way that I promoted and marketed my business. No longer the stealth fighter, I was now a World War II bi-plane soaring overhead, pulling a huge banner with big bold letters: I BUY HOUSES. What will you do?

The Power in Numbers

Lastly, I have always been very self-sufficient, and that has historically been an asset. I was extremely surprised to discover that this was actually another hurdle — and it was a big one! I have always asked lots of questions, since my belief is what I know isn't as important as my ability to find out. But while I asked a lot of questions, I never asked for the opinions and assistance of others unless I had a specific question. I simply found a solution when one was needed.

Since it was only using my point of view, I was dramatically limiting solutions. This became obvious to me when I joined a mastermind group. When we began sharing ideas, different points of view proved invaluable. Superior solutions can be found when everyone works together. As I came to know the members of this group very well, I realized that our power was no longer just the number of the group members times one. Together we became powerful — the number of the group times infinity.

It came as quite a surprise when I realized that I hesitated to discuss my business unless I had a question because I didn't want to waste their time. If I assumed that I was wasting their time, why didn't I ever feel that way about sharing my own time? One day I had an epiphany — I was not only robbing myself of the input that I needed, but more importantly I was robbing them of the joy of sharing their knowledge with me. When I changed this, I started getting solutions to problems that I didn't even know I had.

The best way to avoid this hurdle yourself is to join your local real estate investors club. Within this group, network and find a smaller group of people to form your own mastermind. If there isn't a club in your area, why not create one? I know that's possible, because that's what I did. It isn't that difficult and the rewards are immeasurable.

In closing, there will always be hurdles. I have identified the hurdles that were the most difficult for me to overcome. Your hurdles might be totally different. Some will be very easy to recognize. Others are intangible and invisible. Simply ask yourself, why am I stuck? Why aren't I making the progress I expect? Remember you can go over, under, around or through any hurd — once you have identified it. Navigate the hurdles to success.

May you run a flat out sprint, soaring over the hurdles, never letting them impede your success as you race to freedom!

Krystal Migliore is President of American Rainbow Properties, Inc. located in Gridley, California. The company specializes in solving the problems of distressed homeowners by creating win-win solutions. She is also the founder and leader of the New Real Estate Investors Club Yuba/Sutter. To find out more, call (530) 846-7200 or go online to www.cash-quick-easy.com.

How To Time
The Real Estate Market
For Maximum Gains!

by David Lindahl

When you mention market timing, most people think of the stock market. But what if I told you that you could become wealthier, faster if you learned to recognize which phase of the cycle any real estate market is in and then based your buying and selling decisions to maximize the advantages of each cycle?

What if you discovered that, if you learned to recognize just one particular phase of these cycles and only invested in markets that were in this one phase, you would be literally guaranteed to obtain the maximum amount of success? We are talking here about millions of dollars in a very short amount of time.

Read this chapter to its very end and you will realize how to do just that.

There are two types of real estate investors: institutional investors and entrepreneurial investors. Entrepreneurial investors are people like you and me who buy real estate and either flip it for a profit or hold it long term for appreciation and cash flow. The problem with most entrepreneurial investors is they only want to invest in their own "back yard" and they "fall in love" with their properties and hold them forever.

When this happens, their return on equity (the return you are getting from the equity that you have in your property) gets lower and lower as your equity get larger and larger.

Most people think that it's good to have a large amount of equity in their properties. What they don't realize is that they could use that equity to acquire larger properties, creating larger cash flows (spendable income) and thus creating even larger and larger equities.

The institutional investor's entire strategy is based on "rolling" their equity into larger and larger appreciating assets. Doing this allows them to make the most amount of money in the shortest amount of time.

When you as the entrepreneurial investor start thinking like the institutional investor, you begin the journey to attaining enormous wealth. It all begins with understanding the market cycles of real estate and the advantages that multi-family ownership has over single-family ownership.

Before we talk about the different market cycles, let's compare and contrast single-family properties and multi-family properties. Multi-family properties have seven distinct advantages over single-family properties.

They are:
1. Greater Cash Flow
2. Less Risk
3. Economies of Scale
4. Less Competition
5. Ability to Hire Professional Management
6. Bigger Pay Days
7. Easier to Get the Money

1. Cash flow on a multi-family property is always greater than that of a single-family. Simply put, more units means more rents coming in. Your average unit may bring in a profit of $300 per month. If you have one unit (a single-family) that's only $300 per month. If you have 10 units, that's $3000 per month. Hmmm, let's see … $300 or $3000? That's a no-brainer!

2. The more units you have under one roof, the less risk you have. If you have a single-family house and you lose your tenant, you've lost 100% of your income. In some instances, this could be your entire profit for the year. If you had a ten unit building and lost a tenant, you would still have nine rents coming in to pay your expenses and to give you cash flow (spendable income)!

3. Economies of scale favor the multi-unit buildings. If you have ten single-family houses opposed to one six-family unit, you'll have ten roofs that need to be replaced or repaired, ten lawns to be maintained, and ten tenants spread out throughout your city or town. In your ten-unit building you'll have one roof, one lawn and your tenants are centrally located. Economies of scale favor the more units you have under one roof.

4. There's a lot less competition for the multi-unit buildings than there are for single-family houses. Why? Perhaps because there are not a lot of people out there teaching how to do it, whereas there are plenty of real estate "gurus" making the flipping of single-family houses sound as easy as chewing gum in the dark. The smart investors put multi-units in their portfolios along with single-family houses. (Institutional investors do not hold any single-family houses.)

5. Because of the bigger cash flows in multi-family properties, you can afford to hire management companies to manage your tenants. This eliminates hassle while you go out and do what you do best (or should do best) — finding and financing them (with other people's money). When you are analyzing your multi-family deals, be sure to expense for your management fees. If the property cash flows with management fees expensed, it's a keeper. If it doesn't … go on to the next one. Your time should not be spent unclogging toilets and taking tenant calls. Your time should be spent on those things that make you wealthier … finding more deals.

6. Your paydays are a lot bigger when you finally sell your multi-family property. An apartment complex obviously will cost more than a single-family house. Therefore, they appreciate more as you hold the property. For example, a $100,000 single-family house, in a market that appreciates 10%, will be worth $110,000 while a ten unit property worth $600,000 in the same market (10% appreciation) will increase to $660,000. That's $60,000 more money in your pocket! If you bought both properties with little or no money down, you're much better off owning the ten-unit building.

7. It's easier to get the money for the larger properties. If you go to a bank to get financing for a single-family property, the bank is going to take a good look at you, your history and your credit worthiness. Then they will make a decision based on credit scores and income ratios. When you go to the bank looking to finance large apartment buildings, the bank is concerned primarily about the property — what condition it is in, where it is located, how is the market and, most importantly, is it cash flowing. The bank qualifies the property first and then takes a look at you as an afterthought. Banks even grant "non-recourse" financing. This means that the bank does not require you to sign personally for the loan! Imagine taking out a mortgage on a million dollar property and not being personally responsible!

As you can see, there are many different advantages apartment buildings have over single-family houses. That's not to say to stop flipping single-family houses for chunks of cash! On the contrary, keep getting those chunks. But look to create your real wealth by buying and selling apartment buildings, based on the different phases of the real estate cycle.

There are four major phases of the market cycle:
1. Seller's Market Phase I
2. Seller's Market Phase II
3. Buyer's Market Phase I
4. Buyer's Market Phase II

Each one of these phases has particular strategies that you should be using to maximize your wealth. Using the wrong strategy in the wrong phase could be disastrous.

In a Seller's Market Phase I:

- Property prices are rising
- Rents are rising
- The time that properties stay on the market is near its shortest time of all four cycles
- Employment is growing at a good pace, and
- Demand for property is at its highest point.

Some people think that this is not a good time to be buying. Actually, it's always a good time to be buying real estate, as long as you use the right strategies. This market is the second best market to be buying in. There is still a lot of upside potential in appreciating and rental growth. Demand is at its height so you know that there is going to be someone out there (usually quite a few people) who will want to buy your property. Your strategy in this market is to buy and hold long term, flip or start long-term rehab projects. This is a good market in which to be an investor.

In a Seller's Market Phase II, the market begins to change. This is the riskiest of all four market cycles.

- The time that properties are staying on the market starts to increase.
- Employment begins to slow.
- Demand begins to slow. Sellers are still getting inflated prices but it's taking a lot longer to do so.

Sellers who have their properties on the market begin to realize that the market is changing, so they start to lower their prices to move their property. Investors who were sitting on the sidelines waiting for the market to top off now realize that the market has topped and nervously begin putting their inventory on the market.

This causes the sellers with properties already on the market to lower their prices even more. Buyers begin to realize what is happening and they start to pull back. They begin to make lower offers. There's no more competing for properties. Some take a wait-and-see attitude and leave the market completely, waiting to come back when prices have lowered. This is the beginning of the downward cycle and eventually results in a Buyers Market Phase I.

The strategies of the Seller's Market Phase II is to buy and sell quickly. Flip. If you're going to hold for the long-term, you must be buying properties with a lot of cash flow and a lot of equity. You'll need this to sustain you through the next phase of the market.

You'll want to focus on motivated sellers because most sellers still think they can get the inflated prices of the previous phase. There are not as many deals in this phase but the good news is the deals that you get will have a lot more equity in them. This is because we have just gone through a phase of rapid appreciation.

As we enter the ***Buyers Market Phase I:***
- Prices of properties continue to decline.
- Properties stay on the market for longer and longer periods of time.
- Unemployment reaches its lowest levels.
- The market is now oversupplied with properties.
- Rents are falling and demand for real estate eventually reaches its lowest point.

Contrarian investors feel that this is the best time to get into the market. Their "buy low/sell high" mentality has made many of them very wealthy. However the problem with investing in a Buyers Market Phase I is that you don't know how low the market is going to go down. There is an old adage in real estate investing that says, "Never catch a falling knife." Unless you are aware of changes that are happening in the area that you are interested in buying in, you are primarily investing for cash flow, since there is no appreciation in this market.

You must have enough cash flow to see you through further downturns in the market. When you're flipping properties in this market, you want to base your buying numbers on a resale price that is below market. This is so you can sell the property and get your money back so you can go out and do it again. You'll want to check with the Economic Development Committee in the city that you plan on investing in. Ask them what they are doing to attract new jobs to the area. Jobs are the main reason that a city begins to recover. Usually, cities offer tax incentives and abatements for companies to move to their area.

This creates jobs. With the jobs comes a migration of people. With the people comes demand for apartments. We all know what happens when demand increases …
prices go up. Because we are investing in income properties, this increases the value of our properties. So this is the first sign of a recovering market. It usually takes a company 1–3 years to move. If you know that jobs are coming before anyone else does and you start buying real estate in that area, you are going to hit a home run! This is when you should be investing heavily in a Buyers Market Phase I. As those jobs begin entering the marketplace and the people migrate in, the city begins to enter a Buyers Market Phase II.

In a ***Buyers Market Phase II,*** the market has made the transition.
- Prices are no longer falling; they have begun to slowly increase.
- Rents have begun to slowly increase along with occupancies and job growth.
- Properties that once sat vacant and boarded up are now being rehabbed.

The market is beginning to appreciate and will continue to appreciate at faster and faster rates. This phase is the millionaire maker! When you find a market that is in this phase or recognize that your city is in this phase, you want to scoop up as many properties as you can! In a very short time of holding these properties, you will be financially set up for life! This is the market that we at www.rementor.com specialize in locating throughout the United States.

The strategy when buying properties is to pay the seller at or close to asking price. No need to haggle. As long as the property is cash flowing, your rents and property values are about to take off! Remember, the bigger the property you own, the more money you are going to make in appreciation. People local to the market are usually unaware of what is going on. All they know is that they have been in a buyers market for the last number of years and have been having a hard time selling properties. They are happy to sell to you and sometimes think you are crazy for buying! There is a general pessimistic attitude by the locals in the market. This is good!

If you live in a market that is in a Buyers Market Phase II, after you acquire all of your properties, you'll watch your rent rolls get higher and higher. You will create massive passive spendable income in a very short time. People have retired in five years or less as multi-millionaires, simply living out their days cashing their profits checks. If that is your goal, good for you! However, once you realize how to play this game, you may want to seek other markets around the country and start investing in them. After you experience rapid appreciation and passive income, it becomes addictive. And since you know how to do it, why stop?

You may now decide to take some of your equity out of this market and put it into another market that is just at the beginning of the Buyers Market Phase II phase. At any give time there are 20 – 30 markets around the United States — regardless of what the national economy is doing — that are in the beginning phases of a Buyers Market Phase II. Doing this will compound that equity and make you wealthier and wealthier. We call this "Market Hopping." It is a fast track to becoming rich.

This is how the process works. Locate a market in a Buyers Market Phase II. Accumulate as many properties in that market as you can until the Buyers Market turns into a Sellers Market Phase I.

Remember, this is the phase when demand is at its highest. Hold the property and continue to accumulate properties through this phase, but be more selective in the properties you are buying because some of the "upside" has been taken out of the market. Continue to hold until you see the market start to transition to a Seller's Market Phase II. This is when you sell and invest all of your new found equity into another market. Is there still upside in the market? Sure there is, but you want to have a little "meat left on the bone" for the next investor. "Pigs get slaughtered."

You want to be able to sell the property in a reasonable amount of time because you're taking your profits out from this market and putting them into another market that is poised to take off.

If you try to hang around a market until all the upside has been taken out, you risk not being able to unload your property and then having to hold it through another complete cycle. The average cycle lasts from 8–20 years!

Does Donald Trump only invest in New York City? No. He buys and builds all around the U.S. depending upon the market cycles. Did you know that his first deal was a multi-unit complex that he bought in Ohio? Why? Because it cash flowed and it was in a Buyers Market Phase II.

Start thinking like an institutional investor. Use the strategies of the market cycles when you are buying in your own back yard and you will become wealthier faster. Trump said it best: "If you are going to think, you might as well think big!"

David Lindahl, also known as the "Apartment King" has been successfully investing in apartment buildings and single-family homes for the last eight years. He is the author of four popular, money-making home study courses "Apartment House Riches," "How To Estimate And Renovate Houses For Huge Profits," "Managing For Maximum Profits," *and* "The Real Estate Investors Marketing Tool Kit." *E-mail now for the Free tape* "How To Create A $9700 Monthly Passive Income In 14 Months or Less." *Send your e-mail to Dave@rementor.com today! He can be reached at* dave@rementor.com *and* www.rementor.com.

How To Rake In $1,000 Per Hour in Your Own Home-Based Business
Using No Money of Your Own

by Ted Ciuba

Let me share the honest truth with you. I almost didn't use the above headline. My associates advised me against it. "It just sounds too unbelievable!" they said. However, working part-time, I average over $1,000 per hour of work in my home-based business, using no money of my own. I believe you can, too.

If your goals and ambitions include making big money — really BIG money — FAST, if you would like the personal freedom, self-respect, and community prestige that accompany competent performance, and if you would like to have it happen quickly, without taking any risks or spending any of your own money, read this article thoroughly. It will show you how to have all this and more.

The Opportunity of the 21st Century

I want to introduce you to a truly revolutionary method of making massive amounts of money in short periods of time, at no risk, using other peoples' money. Case in point:

Greg Chaffin earned an amazing $18,695 his first 5 weeks

"Paper" offers you a unique angle to the real estate game. I know of no other opportunity that can offer such large-scale rewards so easily with no risk. And the little guy can still do it! Realistically, if you put dedicated effort into it, full-time or part-time, you can earn $10,000 or more per month.

One Midland, Texas associate, who preferred not to be identified (doesn't want his client to see) pulled in **$9,050 profit on his very first deal.** It can get better than that! **Scott Pentecost**, from New Whiteland, Indiana doesn't mind if I identify him, because he's *bragging*!

> *"I am writing to inform you of the outcome of my first note transaction …
> a spread of $42,696.15!*

I am also writing to say thank you for providing me the opportunity to be successful in the note business. Without your valuable information and guidance I don't think I could have handled such a large transaction, especially for my first note transaction."

You can do this from your home, with no overhead. Put all this together and it's easy to see why insiders call this **"the business opportunity of the 21st Century."** Simply put, the paper business is buying and selling "seller carryback notes" — **mortgages, trust deeds,** and **land contracts**. These liens are generated when sellers carry back all or a portion of financing when selling their residence, rental, or commercial property.

Actually, it's more than just mortgages and trust deeds — you can also buy **annuities, structured settlements, lottery winnings,** and **property leases**. Your profits on these "cash flow instruments" can be as great or greater than your profits on mortgages. One of our Florida students caught a quick $12,521 brokering an annuity the very first time he did it! Due to space restrictions, we'll only be discussing real estate paper in this article.

The Size of the Market

The market is huge. In fact, other than food and clothing, can you think of anything that every person in this vast country, in one form or another, is involved with all their lives? Housing! And one in four home sales involves some type of seller financing!

In the eighties we had high interest rates. With the nineties came the great savings and loan crisis. Now we're in the 21st Century, and interest rates are fluctuating … But we still haven't found that people always have all the money they need, have we? There's a tremendous pool of seller carryback mortgages, and it's filling faster than we can drain it.

"Why Would Someone Sell a Note at a Discount?"

Because they want or NEED money. Perhaps they feel burdened with the responsibility of owning a note. Sometimes they don't feel good about waiting for another person to pay them. Perhaps other opportunities are taking their time. Perhaps they have a medical emergency … . Whatever the reason, they want cash now rather than a trickle over forever.

"Where Do I Get My leads?"

All these transactions are recorded at the courthouse. However, searching them out is L-A-B-O-R-I-O-U-S! We can show you how to uncover thousands of leads to follow up. And you sure **won't be wasting your days at the courthouse!** There are services that sell them to you for pennies!

84

Your Profit Opportunities

Our industry is unregulated! Believe it! We make "obscene" profits banks and S&Ls can't touch. But then, we don't "loan" money. We purchase notes created in the sale of real estate, otherwise known as purchase money mortgages. We have an almost unfair advantage over the uninformed unintentional ex-homeowners who carried back a note and really wanted — and still want — cash. There is no "note market."

No one can call their broker and request the going rate on their note. And there are so few purchasers of seller carryback mortgage notes that potential sellers will be glad to hear that you can help them.

There's not a state in the union you can't buy notes in. There are differences in the security instruments and the foreclosure procedures associated with different states, but the differences are minor. Plus, this won't be your problem. Doing things the way we show you, you'll pass these expenses off to the end buyer. Money is no problem in this business. There's a network of billions you can plug into. Easily. Honestly, you can't run out of money for your good deals.

The Two Ways to Make Mountains of Money

There are two main ways you make money — "flipping" or "investing."

Flipping

When you flip a note, you have it sold before you buy it! You do what we call a "double simultaneous contingent close." What this means is that both the purchase of the note from the seller and the sale of "your" note to the end buyer happen at exactly the same moment. You make your money on the spread.

Example: Sally Seller sold her home a year ago. She wanted cash, but the house just wouldn't sell. Bobby Buyer gave her a $25,000 down payment, money he received from the sale of his own home:

$100,000   Purchase
  25,000   Down
  75,000   Carryback

Now Sally needs money. She wants to tour ancient Egypt. She has discovered a mortgage is NOT like money in the bank. She can't just withdraw the principal balance, even though she's willing to accept a substantial penalty for early withdrawal.

You get her info and discover you can sell her note for $70,114. You ring her happily announcing you can get her $62,250. When she accepts, you've just put the difference, $7,864, into your own pocket!

This scenario describes a transaction with a year's "seasoning," but this same process can also be accomplished "simultaneously" with the purchase and sale of the property.

Your total time in this deal might hit 3 hours. That's $2,621.33 per hour.

> "I made about $1,900 on my first deal and was able to pay my tuition at Loyola with it. It feels good!" — Lori Zoila

> Christian Naef wanted to brag a bit. So he sent me a fax of his high deal to date: $17,000 profit on a single note deal!

Actual results depend on you. You may do better or worse than the above examples. Once you go full-time, you may be doing 3–6 per week. Isn't that wealth?

Investing

Most people enter this business for the fast cash profits they can make using other people's money. However, it doesn't take too many deals to pay off your debts, purchase new cars, a new house, and send the kids to school. You will be looking for investment opportunities. There is no investment more secure than real estate backed paper. You buy these notes for pennies on the dollar. Additionally, you seldom buy a note that backs 100% of the property.

Let's say you get involved in the following:

$165,000	Original sales price
45,000	Down
120,000	Seller carryback

(15 year, 12%, $1,440.20 payment)

This interest rate, for the benefits of seller financing, is normal. Over time, being in a desirable neighborhood, the value of the property increases slightly to $180,000. Not only that, but the prudent payor has taken advantage of the no prepayment penalty clause, and has paid the loan down to $89,000. Two years later, when the noteholder needs cash rather than $1,440 monthly, the loan-to-value ratio is only 49%.

But wait! You don't purchase the note for the principal balance owing. You offer $65,000.

So what do you have now? What kind of return are you making? You've just picked up a note with 97 payments remaining. (Term shortened due to principal paydown.) Your return is 22.04%.

Early Payoff

However, in this society where 25% of the population moves every year, it's likely you will get paid off early. Magic! Let's say one year after you invest in the note the payor moves into another house, selling his old home and paying off your note in the process. The payoff would be $82,022. Your annual return, with the payments and the payoff, exceeds 47%!

Foreclosure

It can get better. You have a $65,000 security lien on a $180,000 home. If a year later the payor was to default, and you "got" to foreclose you would make some serious money! (Foreclosure is a very simple and painless procedure on your part. The big "secret" is to have professionals do it.)

Because you hold the first lien, even if there is a second and/or third behind you, you get the entire property free and clear! You just made $115,000! Not counting the payments you received, that's a 106.3% return!

Hypothecation

What if you don't yet have $65,000, but you encounter this sweet deal? Simple — hypothecate. This is a banker's term for borrow.

Certain financial institutions and hoards of private investors would see its value. They would give you the money to purchase this note. Now they want to make money, so they charge you 8.5% interest. (Remember, they are conventional lenders, and they've got a 51% protective "no-lose" cushion. Your monthly payment is $1,287.95.

But, let's look at what you've done with no money out of your pocket:
$1,440.20   monthly payment from payor
$1,029.37   your monthly payment to bank
$410.83   monthly spread — PURE PROFIT

Before you laugh at $410.83, remember we're looking at this from the investing point-of-view. Some would say it's better to flip it and get a quick $7,864 — and if you need the money, no doubt about it. However, the monthly income is kool, and on the 7 years of this note, you'll actually earn $34,509.59.

Then you'll own the mortgage "free and clear" and get six more years of $1,440.20 per month. That's an additional $103,694.40. Total them together and that's $138,203.99. This is 100% profit on a **ZERO** investment. (Return-on-investment = infinite!) Those are wealth rates of return.

www.mentorsmagazine.com

And your personal financial situation makes no difference. Unlike a normal loan, you are not the one they are looking to for repayment of the loan. Even though you are buying the carryback, they will look to the payor and the property.

What if you had 10 of these? What if, after doing this business for five years you had 35 like this? $410.83 x 35 = $14,379.05. **Could you live on $14,000 of management-free monthly income?!**

Let's Sum Up

This is America's perfect home-based business. Part-time or full-time, the only thing you need to start earning massive income is specific knowledge and your telephone.

Your income is limited only by the number of deals you do. There is a vast market of sellers, more than you could ever contact. And they are everywhere. Getting money is no problem. There's literally billions of dollars at your beck and call.

You can live anywhere and do this business. Every community has seller carryback paper.

If you've ever run a business before, you'll really appreciate the fact there's no inventory, no employees, and no store or warehouse space. These gigantic overhead expenses — continuing whether sales justify it or not — have ruined many small businesses.

If you're ready to change your life, this is your time. Discover the paper market.

*To discover more about the exciting "paper" business, surf to www.realprofit.com/paper or call 615-780-2960 for a free special report. To contact author & note investor **Ted Ciuba** directly, call 615-662-3169 or write tedc@realprofit.com*

Create Your Own Garden of Eden!

by Larry & Sharon Yelinek

We have lived as a blended family for the last 25 years. I (Larry) brought five children to our family, three boys and two girls, and Sharon brought two sons. These seven children have blessed us with 17 grandchildren and six great grandchildren. We started our real estate business after we were great grandparents. We had no retirement program and lost most of our life savings in a failed business venture. I was self-employed most of our marriage and loved every moment of it, but I was always looking for something … not quite knowing what it was I wanted. Sharon worked at various jobs during our first 25 years together.

Watching late night television one night, I bought a course regarding investing. Sharon would not look at the material. She did not want anything to do with real estate. She only asked, "How much did it cost?" That course was the first step in an education that has paid the price of that course many times over. I finally realized what I had been looking for all this time: real estate investing! A friend of mine told me about a FREE three-day seminar coming to town. Since I wanted to get into investing, why not call? Sharon came with me. After maxing out our credit cards to go to this FREE seminar, we decided we wanted to try Pre-Foreclosure.

It took us another six months before we really started. Over the next few months, we bought seven houses, acquired with $10 each, out of our pocket. No one even checked our credit. Closing was done within a few hours after seeing the house. The value of each house was from $100,000 - $280,000. After being successful at Pre-Foreclosure in the first year, we decided to branch out to other areas. Little did we realize what we would be doing in the next year!

After six months working in the real estate investing business, we attended another FREE seminar. This time we invited several people to meet at a restaurant and talk about successfully buying houses. We had eighteen show up for the first meeting! We decided to meet again, so we set it up for the following month to see if the pep talk helped. Within the next six to seven months, we had around 45 people attending and had to move to a new location. This new location held 80 people, but the first night there was standing room only. Several investors left because there was no room. We moved again, this time to a hotel.

We now run one of the largest private real estate investor groups in Michigan. The meeting now provides networking, with investors from many areas in the business. The group draws national and international speakers monthly.

We bring to the table accumulated knowledge of the members that ask and answer questions at the monthly meeting, and even better questions on the phone or over private lunches with members. Many people ask us how they could learn the cookie-cutter approach we use to buy single-family homes. After having lunch and dinner regularly with people, and finding each person asking the same questions, it was time to prepare a Pre-Foreclosure Boot Camp. We had 18 people sign up for our very first one! What a rush it was for us! These people were looking to us for direction, but we found that every time we helped someone, we learned from them. This still happens to us today!

At a Boot Camp, the time in class will make you work on the things that get the telephone ringing with very motivated sellers. We visit the local County Building to learn how to look up records, and we visit the location of the Sheriff's Sale. We cover how to get the home visit and the two-step close that gets the house under contract. Speaking of contracts, they are covered in detail!

Two times a year, we deliver a two-day Short Sale Boot Camp, which follows the Pre-Foreclosure Boot Camp. That way, if someone was making a trip from out of the area, both camps could be done in one trip to beautiful Michigan!

The key to success in real estate investing is getting your education. Build a team that consists of a CPA, lawyer, realtor, banker, title company, investing partners, a mentor and a coach. Your investment group is the first place to begin building your team. You need that group to find most of them.

Starting an Investors Club

An investors club draws all the team members to one room on a given day. Everyone comes to the meeting looking to make their dreams come true. Everyone wants to talk to the leader of the group. As the leader of a group of investors, many deals are brought in for advice or coaching. Some of them can become 50/50 to 75/25 partnerships.

Many late night television ads are drawing new potential members every week. They buy the tape set(s) and think they are now ready to begin. Sure! Most of us who are making good money in real estate investing did not stop with one book or tape set. Each month, an investors club offers more education to the members. With the speakers that an investment club can bring to their members and to the public, the opportunities to learn are staggering. As the leader of the club, you can have your own members talk and show the others what they are doing, or you can bring in other speakers, whether national or international. However, never forget to get the people at the meeting involved before you have the main speaker talk. People like to hear what others are doing and how they did it!

Do You Want a Coach and Partner to Form a Club in Your Area for You to Garden?

The best success tool for the greatest wealth stream of all is education. There are slow ways to grow your wealth, or ways to make your club grow in the hothouse of fresh deals every day. There are keys to growing a club even when there are strong real estate investing groups in the area. Potential mentors, partners and coaches have done what you want to do. Tapping into the wealth of their knowledge is the fast track to success!

Platform Speakers Try Outs Available

Real estate investors are a group of people willing to buy "How To" investing courses. Many people who read this book already know their niche. We encourage you to follow, and cash in on the great rewards of owning and running a club. When a successful investor has a knack to teach clubs, speaking engagements are the next step. Running a club means needing speakers. This is of utmost importance to a promoter! Your job becomes locating platform speakers (teachers) from all over the world to teach the strategies to make and preserve income.

The Garden of Eden is the best place for fresh first time investors. Since you are reading this far in this book, you will stick to the New Real Estate Investors program. If you have a niche product and are interested in promoting it, send Larry & Sharon Yelinek the info and let's talk about speaking at one of our clubs around the country!

New Real Estate Investors LLC Mission Statement:

"To Assist Its Members In Succeeding In Their Real Estate Investment Plans By Providing Continuing Education, Motivation, And Opportunity In A Positive And Mutually Supportive Environment."

www.NewRealEstateInvestors.com

Larry & Sharon Yelinek offer the fast track plan of providing continuing education, motivation, and opportunity in a positive and mutually supportive environment. When you are ready to fast track to new heights, contact Larry & Sharon Yelinek and let us talk about creating your own Garden of Eden. Email LarryYelinek@hotmail.com or Larry@NewRealEstateInvestors.com or Sharon@NewRealEstateInvestors.com

Do You Need a Website for Your Real Estate Investing Business?

by Alex Galitsky

When we start or grow our Real Estate Investing business, we are faced with many decisions. We decide which courses we want to invest in, which seminars we want to attend, and what tools we need in order to gain an edge over our competition.

Techniques Improve with Time

Chances are, the way things were done a few years ago have been improved upon. If you do the same old thing while your competition is using improved techniques, you will be less efficient and may soon be out of business. In order to stay competitive, you must always tweak your business and adapt it to the fast, ever-changing investing world.

Use Timesaving Tools

One of the hottest tools used by Real Estate Investors right now is a database-driven website, which allows easy analysis and follow-up with prospects. It also allows easy access to checklists and the right paperwork to get the deal done right as efficiently as possible. It is like having your own Real Estate Investor's Office at your fingertips.

Imagine if handling *sellers* was as easy as this: A seller calls your answering service, and the answering service goes through the seller questionnaire, and e-mails you the lead. The lead is automatically inserted into the database of your website. You power up your laptop or PDA, and connect to the internet via wireless network. You log in to your own Real Estate Investor's Office, where you can instantly analyze the lead and create possible offers.

Handle Buyers Efficiently

Imagine if handling *buyers* was as easy as this: A buyer calls your answering service. The answering service goes through the seller questionnaire, and e-mails you the lead. The lead is automatically inserted into the database of your website. You power up your laptop or PDA and connect to the internet via wireless network. You log in to your own Real Estate Investor's Office, where you can instantly analyze the lead and determine which houses from your inventory the buyer qualifies for. If none, they will stay in the system and you can possibly offer them another house in the future if you find one that will get them qualified.

Have Confidence

Do you think you will have more confidence to advertise, because you know you can handle the leads? Sure. Do you think you will be more efficient and have more time to spend with family and loved ones? Sure. The reason why so many real estate investors fail is because they don't do the most important thing and that is to advertise.

I will bet one of the biggest reasons you are not advertising enough is because you don't have a system in place to handle the leads effectively. You know that you will not get the full value out of your advertising dollars if you don't handle the leads properly.

Plan for Success

If you are serious about Real Estate Investing, or if you just value your time, you need to invest in one of these websites. In the space permitted, I can't possibly tell you all about this website, but if you send a blank e-mail to mentors@reioo.com you will get a FREE report sent to you automatically.

Alex Galitsky bought his first property in August 2001. He managed to move his Real Estate Investing career forward and see some success while still working a full-time job as a Software Engineer.

Alex graduated magna cum laude from SUNY at Buffalo and earned a degree in Chemistry and a degree in Computer Science in just four years.

Although Alex enjoys developing software, he no longer works full-time as a Software Engineer. His focus now lies primarily in Real Estate Investing and on managing a team of developers to make the www.reioo.com the most useful Real Estate Investor's Online Office. Send a blank e-mail to mentors@reioo.com to get a FREE report.

A Powerful
Mindset Strategy
to Grow your
Real Estate Business

by Eric Lofholm

For the last eleven years I have been searching for the finest ideas on sales and success. *The Mastery Strategy* is one of the simplest, most profound ideas I have ever discovered. For most people this one idea, when implemented, will dramatically increase their performance!

Most people just learn enough to get by when it comes to their business and personal development skills. For example, their time management skills are strong enough to get by. Negotiation skills, follow up skills, and rapport skills are strong enough to get by. They have not yet committed to mastering any of these skills.

Let me start by sharing what mastery isn't. Mastery is not a goal or a destination. It is not something that you achieve. It is a philosophy. It is an approach to life and business. To me, mastery is lifelong pursuit of excellence. Mastery is a path that leads to the highest level of achievement.

Think of a martial arts master. This is a person who has dedicated his life to excellence. There was a turning point in the martial arts master's life that happened long before he or she became a master. The turning point came when the master was much younger. The turning point was the moment when he or she made a decision to become a master. In that one moment, the future master made a decision to get on the path to mastery and stay on it. What could happen if you made a decision to become a sales master today? George Leonard wrote an excellent book called *Mastery*. I highly recommend it.

Your mind is designed to answer whatever question you ask yourself. For example, if you ask yourself, "What is my favorite beverage when I wake up in the morning?" your brain will answer that question. You will probably get an answer like coffee, tea, or orange juice. Your brain will answer business questions as well. Here are a few examples:
  1. How could I reach my goals even faster?
  2. How can I double my results working half as many hours?
  3. How can I double my net worth in the next 12 months?

94

I have asked myself hundreds of business questions. The following question is the most powerful sales question I have ever discovered. *What is the one selling skill, that if I mastered, would increase my results the most?* Your brain will answer this question. You get what you focus on. By focusing on mastering this skill your results will, in most cases, dramatically increase.

Where did the question come from? I read an article about Tiger Woods a few years ago. The title of the article was, "How the Best Golfer in the World Got even Better." During Tiger's rookie year he won over $60 million in prize money and endorsements. At the Masters in his second year he won the tournament by a record 12 strokes! After winning the Masters, Tiger watched videotape of the tournament with his coach. Even though Tiger had won by a record margin, he and his coach both agreed he had not yet mastered his swing. On that day Tiger made a decision to master his golf swing. Over the next 18 months, he only won one tournament. The press wondered if Tiger would ever be a great golfer again. Then, one day, it all came together. Tiger won 10 out of 14 tournaments. Then he won the 4 major tournaments in a row. This feat had never been accomplished in the history of golf. He was able to accomplish this because of his commitment to mastering his golf swing.

Ask yourself the mastery question: what is the one skill that if I mastered, would increase my results the most?

1. Make a decision to master that selling skill.
2. Develop an action plan to become a master of that skill.
3. Take action on your plan.

The Mastery Strategy will work for you. Don't wait another second to take action. Grab a pen and paper right now and ask yourself, "What is the one skill that if I mastered, would increase my results?" After you have identified the skill, make a decision right now to get on the path to mastery. The decision that you just made will impact your results for the rest of your life. I look forward to meeting you at a future seminar.

Eric Lofholm is the president of Eric Lofholm International, Inc., a global sales training company. The company headquarters are in San Diego, California. His phone number is (888) 81-SALES. To receive a free copy of Eric's book, 21 Ways to Close More Sales Now! *go to www.ericlofholm.com. Eric can be reached by email at eric@ericlofholm.com*

Multiple Streams of Motivated Sellers

by Richard Roop

Finding great deals is one of the toughest jobs for an investor. That's right. Raising cash or finding a "quick turn" buyer is easy on killer deals. The market is full of bargain hunters and private investors who have money. So the real key to investment success is finding properties you can pick up at a great price or with great terms. There are plenty of opportunities if you're willing to do what it takes to find deals. But some methods require more grunt work than others. And frankly, I'm lazy.

I discovered long ago that I preferred having sellers call ME... I don't like knocking on doors unannounced. In fact, I'd never do that. I won't call on "for sale by owner" ads either. Yet … both are proven ways to locate motivated sellers.

I want sellers asking ME to do business with them. My answer was to learn effective **direct response marketing** techniques and get sellers calling me. This is what I recommend to both new and seasoned investors.

For over four years, my real estate investment company has consistently done at least three or four deals a month. The average profit per house is in excess of $27,000. This is accomplished by …

Marketing Yourself as Serious Homebuyer

You can dramatically improve your chances of achieving your "wealth building" and "cash flow" goals by understanding how direct response marketing can help you leverage your time, money and efforts. Did I say I was lazy? It's true. We never go out and hunt for good deals … and rarely do I ever buy a house listed with an agent. We focus on getting sellers calling us who like the idea of a quick and easy sale.

Effective marketing is the process of delivering a series of well-crafted MESSAGES to the ideal MARKETS using "multiple streams" of low cost MEDIA. I'll expand on that formula in a moment. First, let's explore the unique benefits of using this approach to find great deals.

Advantages of Having Sellers Call You

- Everyone you talk to will be pre-screened. That means they own a house, they are thinking of selling and are motivated enough to respond. You leverage your time by speaking only to pre-screened prospects and buying a higher percentage of the houses you find for sale.

- You can educate the seller on the specific benefits you can offer BEFORE they call. You'll spend less time repeating yourself.

- You eliminate the need to call sellers. You might normally chase after sellers with a sign in their yard … an ad in the paper … an expired listing … or their name on a foreclosure list. But now they are calling you instead.

- You'll talk to sellers who haven't done anything to publicize their desire to sell. That means less competition and bigger profits.

Developing a Powerful Marketing Strategy

As we walk through this process, I'll include some special web links where you can get more instruction or see examples. These tools are on my free marketing website for real estate investors. You'll discover a wealth of articles and streaming online audio revealing little known "sledgehammer" techniques. Tapping into these resources will help you more easily apply these ideas to your own operation. I created this website to help you buy and sell houses with little or no money down … without getting loans from banks … without the need for agents … and without relying on mortgage brokers to perform.

It surprises me to meet so many real estate investors who are oblivious to the proven strategies readily available for acquiring dozens of houses without using their credit or making large down payments … without struggling with tenants … and without fixing houses. But I can't imagine operating any other way!

How to Get the Right Message to the Right Market at the Right Time

Now we'll explore the three M's of direct response marketing for real estate entrepreneurs … identifying who is your Market, creating a compelling Message and then testing various types of Media proven to work best for investors.

1. Clearly identifying your MARKET

Ask yourself these questions. Then I'll give you my answers for buying and selling single family homes.

Who do you want to communicate to?
We want homeowners only … preferably with a house for sale.

Who can you help the most?
We're looking for flexible and motivated sellers.

Who's most likely to need your help?
Some obvious prospects may include property owners dealing with: extensive repairs, too much debt, foreclosure, bankruptcy, divorce, job transfer, probate, bad tenants, etc.

Where do you want to buy?
I suggest "farm" specific neighborhoods or parts of town where you can become a *big fish in a small pond.* There are some super advantages of targeting the same 25,000 homeowners five times (over a period of time) than promoting yourself to 125,000 homeowners just once. The cost is the same but the response will be dramatically different when a prospective seller sees what you have to offer numerous times.

What types of property to target?
I prefer casting a wide net for single family homes because they are plentiful and in high demand. Other more specialized niches you can attempt to target include ugly houses (they need lots of work), luxury homes (if you know your exit strategy), multi-family properties, newer homes in newer subdivisions, etc.

2. Creating a MESSAGE that matches your market

Here are some of the elements to include in your marketing message followed by examples for buying single family homes.

What are the top benefits can you offer the seller?
Fast cash, fair price, quick closing, instant debt relief.

Why should they choose you over the other options they have to sell their house?
Avoid putting house on the market, avoid a buyer backing out at the last minute, sell "as is" without fixing up a property to show, avoid becoming an unwanted landlord if it doesn't sell fast enough.

What are the most important benefits you can offer to a seller?
Enjoying peace of mind, avoiding uncertainty, making the whole process easy.

What problems can you help a seller overcome?
Avoid foreclosure, avoid bankruptcy, avoid double house payments, avoid relying on an agent to perform.

Why is it easy and safe to do business with you?

Include testimonials, organizational affiliations, recognition by local media, actual real life examples of how you helped others … and any other proof that you're a professional who delivers on your promises.

Why should they call you now?

"Call me first and you still have all your other options available if I can't make you an acceptable offer. Imagine, your house could be sold by this time next week."

What do you want them to do next?

Go online and submit property information, call an operator 24 hours a day to submit property information, call to learn more and take the next step, complete the enclosed form and fax now, mail in the enclosed postcard, call a 24 hour recorded message to learn more, request a free special report, etc.

3. Proven, cost effective MEDIA to get your message delivered

Classified Ads

The structure of a classified ad is a headline with a few benefits and a call 'o action. Look for publications that reach your "farm" such as daily newspapers, weekly papers, shopper magazines, etc. Consider using a "two-step" approach by incorporating a 24-hour recorded message line or website and then systematically deliver more information and benefits … automatically. Go to www.richardroop.com/frm2buy to hear my free recorded message for buying houses.

Display Ads

For small display or space ads, use the same type of message as in a classified ad. If cost effective (usually if the publication has a lower circulation), place up to full-page ads to get a very detailed message out in one shot. Directory ads such as in the phone book can be great once you're ready to commit for a year.

Flyers

You can get your entire message on a full-page flyer. Sell the other side to a non-competing business and cut your costs in half. Or use the other side to solicit new home buyers or tenants. These can be distributed in many ways; my favorite is to have them inserted in newspapers.

Signs

Yard signs, pole signs, vehicle skins and billboards all work well. Go to www.richardroop.com/signs for web links to affordable sign providers and to see examples of my yard signs and billboards.

Web Site & Email

These days, if you're not using a web site to distribute your marketing message, to gather info and to build credibility, you're working too hard. If needed, hire someone to help you with it. Go to www.richardroop.com/webtools for a list of "real estate investor website" providers.

Free Special Reports

An awesome technique is to have a sales letter that includes ALL the elements of your marketing message as discussed in step 2. This will be the same message used in large display ads, web sites or flyers. Beef it up with anything that would give you credibility. Now you have a Free Special Report. Offer to mail it in your 2-step advertising. Or use it as a "leave behind" when visiting prospective sellers. I mail one to a seller on the same day they call me … whether I have an appointment or not. It's a super strategy.

Letters

Nothing beats letters mailed to a highly targeted market. Write out your marketing message in a personal tone. Do everything to make your letter look personal, as if you sent it to just one person. Handwritten is best but a "typewriter look" also works great. Download a free "old typewriter" font and read my article on how to design letters at www.richardroop.com/letters.

Postcards

This is my favorite media because it is cheap and easy. Postcards do not have to look personal but should have a big, bold compelling headline. Use the same headline from your classified ad, display ads, flyer and free special report. You can systematically print and mail regular postcards for about 24 cents complete (when normal postage alone is 23 cents today) by using the service offered by the U.S. Postal Service. Go to www.usps.com. I also have a system where you can mail large, oversized postcards for just 30 cents complete. These are big enough in include your full flyer message, free special report or lengthy sales letter. Go to www.richardroop.com/ultimate for a free article on how to do this step-by-step.

Business Cards

Always have a 2-step marketing message on your business cards. Carry 10 cards every day and make sure you come home with none. Read "How to Attract Business Using $100 Bill Business Cards" at www.richardroop.com/bizcards.

Other Types of Media

The list is long and I recommend you start with the examples above first. However, there are other ways to get your message delivered to your market: faxes, seminars, door knocking crew, radio, TV, advertising specialties, outbound calls, etc.

To summarize, your goal should be to develop the most comprehensive marketing **message** possible. Intend to communicate everything that would be of interest to your targeted **market**. Tell the whole story. Deliver the entire message when the **media** is cost effective … as with a detailed flyer, free special report or personal looking letter. If that is cost prohibitive, use a two-step approach whereby prospects contact you and then they can get "the rest of the story" by calling a free recorded message, visiting your web site or ordering a free special report.

The Bottom Line

Most beginning investors have more time than money... and a marketing plan requires a regular investment of marketing dollars. You can call sellers and knock on doors for free. And during the startup stage of your business, that's OK. But...consider this. A $15,000 profit from buying and selling ONE house can fund all your marketing efforts for an entire YEAR, even if you're spending up to $800 per month.

If you know how to solve sellers' problems by buying their houses creatively, apply some of these ideas to buy *more* houses with *less* work and make *more* money.

Known as "The Marketing Consultant for Real Estate Entrepreneurs," **Richard Roop** *is an active investor who has completed over 200 deals near his home in Colorado. He's also dedicated to sharing his marketing expertise with real estate investors nationwide. Tap into his free marketing tools, articles and streaming audio at www.RichardRoop.com*

*How 7 Laws of Loyalty
Turned Around My
Embarrassingly Broke Life*

... And What These Secrets Can Do For You!

by Jeff Kaller

I was voted least likely to succeed — the class clown. I lived under the shadow of my college slogan — "Party 'til you puke!" Dead-end restaurant jobs followed one after another — yet, underneath it all, throbbed a true passion for life. Years later, I was the founder of a company with yearly gross sales exceeding $8 million and recognized as the country's leading expert in buying and selling preforeclosure properties. I owe it all to a personal credo — a belief system which, in its purest form, can be easily written on the back of a napkin:

LOYALTY

In itself, the word "loyalty" is just another word — but it's the way I created unbelievable results in the face of adversity, why I did it, and how you can easily do the same. All of us are bound by a set way of being that comes from a "core" belief system. That belief system creates an outcome whether we want it to or not. I loved my previous life, but economically, I was a walking disaster. After my daughter Allie was born, this way of being was no longer any use to me. Now, at age 38, I've carefully held to my most powerful reasons that I am where I am today.

For you, I've clarified and distilled my personal credo into "7 Laws of Loyalty." I give them to you in hopes that you will utilize them on your life journey. Use them to improve the quality of your life. I promise you, the money will flow, just as it did for me.

Before I begin, it's important to understand that loyalty affects anyone's quality of life in this INTERRELATED MATRIX:
- The income you earn, and the lifestyle you live
- Interaction with partners and business associates
- Opportunities you create for employees
- A strong family "unit" with spouse and loved ones
- Interaction with your customers
- The mentors with whom you surround yourself
- Faith in people, faith in deals outside your comfort zone, spiritual balance

102

There must be a balance of all of these, interwoven together. It's all right that you'll always be striving to coordinate these elements — that's what life and the journey are all about.

LAW #1: Be loyal to the income and quality of lifestyle you desire, and how you want to spend your free time.

You must choose and stay loyal to an income-producing vehicle that can economically support the lifestyle you want. You already know it's not about the money — it's about quality of life.

If running a petting zoo could pay me $50K per month, heck — I'd probably be doing that. Make sure your work turns you on — gets your heart beating and keeps you up thinking late at night. But be careful that what you love also supports the quality of life you desire. Owning goats and sheep for kids to pet and feed ain't gonna buy you an island in the Bahamas — which happens to be my ultimate goal. To make this goal achievable, I've stayed loyal to investing in preforeclosure properties. I'm clear about how I want to spend my time. When working on an important project, I shut off the cell phone and create productive "think time." TV, following the markets, and most news tends to discourage me — I stay away from that crap. Stay loyal and committed to how you spend your time. Stay focused and on track, and this will support the income you want.

LAW #2: Stay loyal to any business partners and associates with whom you have dealings.

I've seen fickle business people chase a dollar so hard they forget that one of the reasons successful companies exist is because of their ability to maintain stable relationships in today's market. No matter what your future plans are, look and stay strong in your work environment relationships. An old boss and/or co-worker may provide an opportunity in the future. In my teaching and real estate businesses, I never break off a relationship with harsh words. Unless someone steals, I've found that most relationships fall aside from LACK OF COMMUNICATION. Start business arrangements with upfront written agreements, communicate expectations clearly, and negotiate what works for both sides, instead of possibly destroying an already deteriorating business relationship altogether. As a side note: get the heck out of soured business very quickly — cut your losses and move on. I once had two business associates embezzle $180,000. I cut ties, never looked back. My best estimate is that I was able to triple the income I lost in half the time.

LAW #3: A loyal leader builds loyal employees and a "Dream Team" to share and execute their personal vision.

If you don't have employees or even ONE person helping to implement your plan, there are only two reasons: 1) There is no need for an employee, or 2) You don't

103

think you can afford one. In a multiple-company environment, I must have people to ensure that operations get done. As a general rule, one of the most important attributes to growing any company, in my opinion, is NOT knowing how to personally do all of your company's operational tasks. It's OK to understand how things work; I just see too many brilliant entrepreneurs handling ALL the details, rather than being able to concentrate and focus on the overall vision.

Operational Managers should be able to keep business functions running smoothly. Get out of their way. Stay out of the unnecessary details that suck your energy. Make sure employees understand the overall vision. I create trust by seeking my employees' opinions and trusting them. My people know how much the company makes in revenue. I also make it completely clear that without my sacrifices, there would not be a company. Praise, rewards, and bonuses create loyalty. If these rewards happen to create envy or greed, then it's time to get this team member out at all costs, and get someone else to support your vision. Be committed to a very specific income that supports your lifestyle, keeping the smallest, most productive "Dream Team" possible to make it happen. For some people, this may be only one Personal Assistant to keep you organized and on track.

LAW #4: A loyal husband and father/wife and mother create the blueprint for a successful business.

I believe alignment in this area of your life will help fix the broken parts. The purpose of any business is to support the creator, and to enhance the quality of life by the freedoms granted by self-employment. Schedule vacations one year in advance, with special pockets of time around these vacations. From the day I met my wife, Sofia, she and I have worked together. After sixteen years, we still haven't killed each other. We forget the business on personal time. I'm committed to take a call from my daughter during any meeting, any time, any place. I take a "Dad & Daughter Trip" with my eight year old, Allie, two weeks out of each year — just she and I. No cell phone — just an exotic getaway such as Costa Rica, Dominica, Nevis, St. Kitts, and this year Kenya and Botswana, Africa. After all, why do we do all of this? Any person, man or woman, who has drifted from the family "unit" can easily regain love just by committing to spend more time enjoying those to whom he or she is connected by marriage or blood.

LAW #5: My customers get the best I can give them. I stay loyal to the reason they became my client in the first place.

In the preforeclosure business, sometimes we find people whose lives are a mess, financially and mentally. During this chaotic time, it's our goal to keep the bank from repossessing their home, and to save their credit. In most cases, we get paid handsomely to do so.

The lender doesn't get another liability on the books. This is an interesting "tug-of-war," but the goal is a win-win at all times. (For a dynamic FREE audio CD discussing a preforeclosure investor's conversation with a homeowner, call 1-800-646-2574, and ask for Alex.) As I teach others to negotiate debt and buy real estate with none of their own credit, money, or liability, my commitment to these customers is that I deliver the best, cutting-edge, underground strategies available in this country.

I'm known as "the kid who created the 'Ninety-Fiver Club™'". This is a conglomerate of people from all walks of life, some with no previous knowledge of real estate, to whom I have given the knowledge and ability to CASH A CHECK FOR $95,000 OR GREATER ON ONE DEAL!! (To see how to become a Member, go to www.mrpreforeclosure.com, and click on "The Ninety-Fiver Club™.") Not only do I understand the inner workings of buying preforeclosures, I thrive on giving these details to others to make a bundle on their own.

In whatever you do, remember that your customer gets value at all costs. Screw this up and you'll fail. Anytime you are able to outperform your competition and your customer hits a home run, GET A KILLER TESTIMONIAL LETTER FROM THEM. "The proof is in the pudding." Don't tell people what you can do — prove it to them. Here's an example:

Hey, Jeff,

I wanted to give you an update on my successes since the August Boot camp in Nashville. Using the negotiation strategies we learned at the Boot camp from MR. X, I was able to negotiate a first mortgage down from $132,000 to $40,000. Your boot camp taught me how to present a short sale offer to the lenders in such a way that it made sense to cut their losses now, and accept my offer.

I met the appraiser at the property and I pointed out everything that was wrong with the house. Thankfully the house smelled like cats, and the 10-15 full litter boxes sure helped. I put the short sale package together, backing up all the information with estimates and pictures, just as we learned in the Boot camp. I even showed them a side-by-side comparison of what the bank would get if they took the property back vs. selling it to me at a discount. The bank jumped at my offer.

Using none of my own money, I hired a contractor to do the minor repairs, put in new carpet and new paint for a total repair bill of just over $20,000. I had a contract to sell the property well before the repairs were even finished. I sold the house for $144,000.

It gets even better ... The house was on a double lot. I sub-divided the lot, and sold that for $32,800 CASH. So I walked away with a profit of $116,415. NOW THAT IS WHAT I CALL A PAYDAY.

I have had several successful short sales in the past, but nothing ever compared to this … and I owe it all to you, Mr. X and an appraiser who doesn't like cats.

Jeff, you promised me that you would change my life, and my entire family is in full agreement that you are truly a man that lives up to his word. THANK YOU!!!

Warmest regards,
Doug N.
Oshkosh, WI

Doug's own words are more powerful than anything I could ever say. By the way, Doug is in "The Ninety-Fiver Club™". Check him out on our website (www.mrpreforeclosure.com).

LAW #6: Employ and stay loyal to a mentor and a carefully chosen group who is willing to support your belief system.

I started my real-estate investing journey when I bought the Carlton Sheets Course "No Money Down." Over fifty houses later I found myself struggling to manage cash-flow, and even lost one of my own houses to foreclosure. Ted Thomas first opened my eyes to debt negotiations. Ron LeGrand pushed me out of my "comfort zone" more than once. Dan Kennedy and Joe Polish have mentored me with marketing ideas worth millions. I seek out the best personal mentors such as these at all costs, paying as high as $10,000 to consult for just a few hours. The list is too long to go on. Was it worth it? You tell me. My goal is to buy a private island in the Bahamas this year. Many of my students and company affiliates will gain use and benefit from doing business with me. Some companies and investors are on their knees eaking out a living. Those around me are talking about creating a lifestyle most people only dream of. I wonder where they got the idea? I take credit for nothing, and I'm no better than anybody else. I will tell you this: I'm on a lifestyle mission, and I am willing to become a mentor to those ready for a change.

I feel so strongly about mentoring, I've seen to it that the Mr. Preforeclosure Organization provides a Coaching Program and high-level consulting, along with Membership Plans, showing people how to work less and make more. These same people are leaving dead-end jobs, and have changed their way of thinking. It's not about money — it's about finding loyal mentors who can inspire you to your greatest achievements.

LAW #7: None of this matters without unstoppable faith.

I believe in people. I think many people try to do the right thing, but also understand that desperate people do desperate things. My goal is to enable people to have dreams, and to avoid the "sheep" who think it's owed to them. I lost patience with that long ago. It's important to personally confide in those around you in an open way. It creates synergy and allows others to take part in their future. Guidance is all good people require. Have you seen Donald Trump's new TV show "The Apprentice?" One of Trump's loyal executives has been with him for over 20 years, and most likely controlled billions with his own decisions. Trump, without question, has faith in key people — this enables his own goals to be realized.

In casual observance over the past five years, I see that those who look for bigger deals not only have more confidence, but are in it less for the money and more for the chase. Thinking in the small, steady paycheck realm is all right, I suppose, but comes from not understanding what is on the other side of the fence. The last couple of years, I've spent much of my time teaching people how simple it is to close bigger deals. Buying and selling $400,000 to multi-million dollar properties is just as easy as a $35,000 house. It takes no money and a lot of faith.

I've seen people traveling down two paths — some folks have faith and a belief system in a Maker in whom they confide in prayer; others don't. As an observer, I see that both parties usually enjoy very similar levels of monetary success. But without a doubt, I see those who are spiritually balanced have a more productive lifestyle, and truly enjoy the journey more than those without spiritual faith.

"Trust God's Authority — not Man's majority."
~Author Unknown~

These are the 7 Loyal Credos that drive me each day, whether working or not. Stop at nothing in your conquest — understand that someone has always figured it out before you. All you have to do is find that person or organization, and employ them to give you what they have. As my special gift to anyone who has picked up this copy of the *Walking with the Wise Real Estate Investor*, I will give you a special deal on our one-time year-end bash where we will have Donald Trump and many other phenomenal personalities in an event destined to effect your lifestyle transformation! Call student services at 800-646-2578. You'll get a very special gift **just for registering!**

Stay loyal to yourself! To your explosive success … .

Jeff Kaller, a.k.a. "Mr. Preforeclosure," is the Founder and President of the Mr. Preforeclosure "How to Leave Your Job in 90 Days" Organization. This company dedicates its resources to making new real estate entrepreneurs outrageously successful through proprietary Seminar Events, Home Study Systems, Mentoring, and Deal Splits — all conducted around the little-known niche of preforeclosure properties.

Find A Tested and Proven System

by Ron Romano

Do not go where the path may lead ... go instead where there is no path and leave a trail." — Ralph Waldo Emerson

While you're pondering that thought, have you ever wondered at or envied the successful lifestyle certain individuals have? We all know someone who just seems to have it all: money, a good family life, beautiful home, membership at the best clubs ... To satisfy our egos, we tell ourselves it was all handed to them, or they got lucky, or they were at the right place at the right time.

While it may be true in a small percentage of cases, the vast majority of those at the top whom we envy are exactly the same as we are. For you to comprehend how easy it is to have the same kind of success, it is critical that you first *open your mind to looking at things in a different way*. Your success is dependent on you leaving the well traveled path followed by the many. The good news is I've watched hospital attendants, bus boys and general laborers achieve amazing success with no more education or "talent" than you or I currently have. The difference is that they have no pre-conceived ideas of what is supposed to work. They are open to trying something different and letting the results dictate future action.

I co-founded Automated Marketing Solutions with my partner, Michael Kowalski. AMS is the North American leader in providing Turn-Key lead generation and client retention systems for all types of businesses and for all types of marketers. (FYI — there is a big difference between a business owner and a marketer — marketers make the most money.) I regularly speak at seminars and conferences, and likewise attend as many marketing seminars as I can to learn who is making money doing what, and to meet the people who are the most successful at teaching others in their field of choice to become wealthy.

Either by luck or by choice, AMS Systems are an invaluable help in this process ... and I can safely say that we have helped hundreds of individuals become millionaires.

www.mentorsmagazine.com

Successful marketers need our stuff to take their businesses to the next level, so I have the good fortune to work the top marketers in the world. They are clients and, in quite a number of instances, joint venture business partners. Working with highly motivated, highly successful individuals on a regular basis allows one to observe commonalities of behavior, the systems they use to create wealth for themselves and how they teach others to implement the same systems and the same philosophy to create wealth for those that want to learn. What I discovered changed my attitude and approach to both my business and personal life — a change that has been a dramatic and positive life changing experience.

Find A Tested and Proven System
&
Imitate Before You Innovate

What I was able to observe was that all these successful marketers had and followed a specific "System." What was really amazing was that for the most part it was the same "System" they all used — they just plugged their STUFF into it. No one bothered to develop their own completely unique "System." That would take way too much time. Besides, if something is working why not use the template-of-success. So they copied "Systems" that successful people had and modified it for their own particular niche.

It was interesting to me that the same "System" approach was universal in its application. You can plug anybody's STUFF into the same system and have the same level of success — that is, as long as you follow all the steps.

Having a system or systemizing what you do gives your earning capacity an exponential factor that could be unlimited. That also means you don't have to trade your time for money — you don't have to be at your office 100% of the time. Most of us have a job we call a business. What we want is a business that allows us to have the lifestyle we want. To succeed at that means we have to create wealth!

Success is a Process, Not a Happening!

A system that is trackable and measurable gives you the luxury of being able to monitor progress. It becomes easier to identify individual areas that aren't performing as planned and to implement adjustments to improve results. You become less dependent on your product or service and become more aware of the process of success. The stress of the unknown is relieved, plans are made with a clearer understanding of what has to be done and a new found confidence emerges within you.

Lesson 1: There are No Failures — Just Poor Test Results!

When I was first told these words by Dan Kennedy, my whole world stopped, and with that a huge burden of the success/failure mentality was lifted from my psyche. Like everyone else, I was constantly comparing the results of the day-to-day activities in my business with what I determined was success. If they weren't up to those standards I deemed myself as failing.

Reality was that although my goals may have been realistic, I did not have a "System" to follow, nor did I understand the process of testing to achieve the desired results. I thought you did something and either it worked or it didn't. If it worked I was a genius and if it didn't, I was a failure! Sitting back and watching the top guys fail or get poor test results with their marketing material. Then make changes that could be tracked, and then achieving better results (the barometer for results is called making money) reinforced my need to implement this type of system.

With my new found wisdom, I could no longer fail. I was testing … and if the desired results were not achieved I could now change one of the variables in the test. Now … at this point in time I was paying more attention to the methodology and systems that my successful clients were using, so what I was testing had a better chance of success. I was also implementing Systems that could track and measure my marketing. I can now test different strategies, concepts, and products knowing that if I don't achieve the results I wanted — the test results were poor — I can consider what to change to improve test results. Or, I can decide if it is worth it to invest more time and energy in that particular project, or if I should invest my energy in something else that would have more favorable test results.

Changing how I was thinking freed me to explore a different approach to my goal of success. So many people limit themselves to their own perception of how everyone else thinks. They believe that, since I think and react in this manner, then everyone must think and react exactly the same way. It creeps into every aspect of their business and personal lives — what they think their customers needs are, how their customers will react to certain kinds of marketing, and even how others perceive their image.

This type of attitude will hold you back and keep you in the same spot, doing the same things over and over again. How can you possibly expect different results?

Why Doesn't Everyone Do This? It's So Easy!

When I first watched the successes of my clients and then experienced how easy it was to have success myself, I was like a caveman experiencing fire for the first time. My immediate thoughts were, "Why doesn't everyone do this? It's so easy!" Like an evangelist I would preach the good word to all my friends, business associates, and anybody else I happened to bump into. To my great surprise and dismay, my words fell on deaf ears. Most thought I was a fanatic.

However, I did learn two very important facts:

1. Most people have preconceived ideas and beliefs that they won't let go of.
2. Very few people are willing to do anything more than what they are currently doing.

If you can run contrary to these two facts, are not afraid to succeed, and can get off your behind to actually do just a little bit more than the next guy, you're on your way to being the one that has it all. The last piece of the puzzle, "The System," is out there waiting for you to copy.

Ron Romano
Automated Marketing Solutions
www.automatedmarketingsolutions.com
1-800-858-8889

Uncovering the Secrets of Marketing to Motivated Sellers

by Kathy Kennebrook

Just a few short years ago, I attended my first real estate seminar and decided this was the business for me. I could do it on my own time and at my own pace — and still make good money. Considering I was still working a full time job, this seemed to be just the scenario for which I'd been looking. One thing the experts taught us in those seminars was that finding motivated sellers was the key to making money in this business.

After spending a number of years in sales prior to becoming a real estate entrepreneur, I knew that when the prospects contact you first, you have a much better chance of making a good deal. At the time I didn't have a lot of money to work with and needed to make every marketing dollar count.

Motivated Sellers are the Key

I discovered the same theory holds true with motivated sellers. A motivated seller is the key to all good deals. If they contact you first, this significantly increases your opportunity to make a profitable deal. There are lots of opportunities for investors who make the effort to find motivated sellers. Some are more labor intensive and time consuming than others. Learning to influence motivated sellers to contact you first will increase your profits, help you to be more successful and most importantly, save you valuable time. One of the primary reasons for failure in this business is trying to deal with unmotivated sellers. It's like trying to push a rock uphill. You spend all your time chasing dead-end leads and getting nowhere. This is discouraging and can cause you to quit the business altogether before you ever get to see the long-term benefits.

Locating these motivated sellers is the key to your success as a real estate investor. Your money is made at the point at which you purchase the property, so an effective marketing plan is essential to your business. The key point to remember is that most sellers are not motivated. The biggest mistake you can make is to try to make a deal with someone who doesn't want to sell to you. As elementary as that sounds, again, that is the key to success: motivated sellers.

The Secret to Great Deals

Effective marketing is the process of delivering your specific message to a targeted audience through the use of various types of media. This method enables you to find the sellers who really need to sell, as opposed to those who just want to sell. When you find the sellers who really need to sell, you'll end up buying a lot more houses at much better prices and terms. The secret to the really great deals is to find them before anyone else even knows about them. A lot of the deals you will find won't be actively marketed. These sellers have a variety of problems they simply don't know how to solve. Their motivation comes in a variety of forms: age, health problems, financial difficulties, change in marital status, liens and judgments, job transfers, landlords who are tired of having their properties abused, change in family size — just to name a few. Other reasons are more directly related to the property itself, such as estates, properties needing extensive repairs, code enforcement violations or properties that have been vacant for a significant period of time.

So, how are you going to find these sellers and how should you market to them? As a real estate investor, you have an array of choices. You can use classified ads, flyers, signage, web sites, business cards, billboards, radio and television ads or direct mail. You should pick at least three to five ways to market your business. Put them to work for you simultaneously in order to promote your business and draw as many different sellers to you within your market. You must understand a seller's motivation for selling a property in the first place. This is important because if you try and reach sellers in only one way, and you don't find a property in a relatively short period of time, you may become discouraged and quit. You really don't want to do this. There is more business out there than you can imagine! Accept the fact that you'll need to do more than distribute some flyers and hope some motivated sellers call you.

One of the first things you'll need to do is identify your market. Decide where you want to buy and what types of properties interest you. Then develop a marketing plan that fits your personal needs and budget. This way, you eliminate the need to call sellers. You want them to call you first. Marketing is a numbers game: the more leads that come in, the more opportunities you'll have to make deals. You won't buy every deal that comes your way, but when you develop an ongoing, producing marketing strategy that brings in quality leads, you'll be able to pick and choose the kinds of deals you want to do.

As a real estate investor, you need to find a seller who is either flexible on the price of the property or on the terms of the sale. If a seller wants full price and all cash for a property, it's almost impossible for you as the investor to make a good deal. The investor who wants to create a win-win deal and make money should be looking for a seller who is flexible on the terms of the sale. Many of the people I direct mail to practically beg me to take their properties off their hands for a variety of reasons. These are the kind of motivated sellers with whom you want to deal.

113

Direct Mail "Cookie Cutters"

The best way I've found to "niche" market to motivated sellers and control the number of leads coming in is through the use of direct mail. The BIG secret to making direct mail successful is to mail the right letter to the right list; then mail to them over and over. As you will discover, given time, almost every potential seller's circumstances change and make them more motivated to sell. You must let the world know you buy real estate. The best thing about doing direct mail advertising is that you can specifically target the types of sellers you want to reach and cultivate quality leads.

I also find these mailings to be very residual. These potential sellers will hold onto your direct mail pieces until their circumstances dictate that they contact you. When they are ready to sell, they will contact you first, especially since they probably haven't had any contact from anyone else. Usually their properties aren't being actively marketed; therefore there is no competition for these deals. In the meantime, you've gained credibility with these sellers by doing repetitive mailings.

The true secret to success is finding sellers who really need to sell. I use different direct mail campaigns to locate different types of motivated sellers: out of state owners, properties quit-claimed from one person to another, expired listings, burned out landlords, and pre-foreclosures, just to name a few. The best part is that you can customize your marketing to reach exactly the kinds of motivated sellers you want to deal with. This is best done by locating mailing lists and refining them to meet your individual criteria, then mailing to them again and again.

Investors often neglect to market to sellers in this way because they think the list is too difficult to get, or they only send the mailings once and quit. These are some of the easiest lists for you to get and it will be very profitable for you to do so. You can go to a list broker or your local property assessor's office and ask them for a list, or you can create the lists yourself. It's fairly easy to do. You can go to the courthouse and research the divorce cases, death notices, liens and judgments, tax liens, marriage licenses, bankruptcies or Lis Pendens, which is the first step toward foreclosure.

Another way to find motivated sellers is to cultivate relationships with individuals who can help you find deals. One way to do this is to send letters to attorneys who handle family law, estate planning and probate law, divorce and marital law, and corporation and business law and let them know you are in the business of buying houses. Once you develop relationships with some of these attorneys, they will call you when they have a client who needs to sell a property quickly. This is just another way to build lead sources using direct mail.

An additional way to find motivated sellers is to write letters to the owners of vacant houses or houses that look like they need a lot of repairs. If you can find the owners of vacant houses, these are usually deals waiting to be made. The harder the owner is to find, the better deal you'll make. There are lots of ways to find the owners of vacant houses, the easiest of which is to simply use a "skip tracer" to locate them for you. You can also work with realtors who can give you expired listings. The longer a house sits without selling, the more motivated the seller will be. If you get expired listings for out of state owners, these sellers are even more motivated. You can often make a deal with a realtor who will supply you with the list. Tell them you will use them to make offers for you, or simply tell them you'll pay them a fee for their services.

Mail these potential sellers a personal looking and sounding letter. Let them know that you are interested in helping them find a solution to their problem. Even if you don't get a response right away, repeat your mailings at least every thirty days until you do get a response. The main reason that direct mail works so well is that you're reaching targeted sellers. You become the seller's first option when they need to sell. Even if you are on a limited budget, direct mail is an excellent source of leads for you since you can buy more houses from fewer leads, thus maximizing your marketing dollars. As your business grows, you can increase the number of mailings you do. You can also target specific neighborhoods or dominate certain parts of town. In doing so, you become a "property value expert" in those areas, which makes the offer-making process that much easier for you.

You will create an ongoing relationship with your target market, which makes it easy for you to follow up with formerly inflexible or unmotivated sellers. Since these mailings are so targeted and so residual, there is virtually no competition for these properties. It puts your lead generating system on "auto-pilot," leaving you more time to make offers, do more deals, and make more money. Most importantly, be consistent in all your efforts. The successful real estate investor has a network of people and strategies at their fingertips at all times. If you don't develop continuity to your marketing campaigns, you'll see your results begin to drop off immediately.

When you learn to get motivated sellers contacting you and then learn a variety of ways to purchase properties, the possibilities become almost endless. When you use several different techniques, you will have more opportunities than you'll be able to handle. Using direct mail to develop a "cookie cutter" system to accomplish this is one of the most affordable, reliable, and effective ways I know to build your business quickly and have all the deals you will ever need. Remember, the key to your success is to find the truly MOTIVATED sellers!

Kathy Kennebrook has actively been investing in real estate since 1999. This 4'11" grandmother is one of the country's leading Real Estate Marketing experts. She currently authors Marketing Magic: How To Find Motivated Sellers, *and* Marketing Magic Spanish Upgrade. *You can visit her at Marketingmagiclady.com.*

The Elements
of the Deal

by Donald Trump

My style of deal-making is quite simple and straightforward. I aim very high, and then I just keep pushing and pushing and pushing to get what I'm after. Sometimes I settle for less than I sought, but in most cases I still end up with what I want.

More than anything else, I think deal-making is an ability you're born with. It's in the genes. I don't say that egotistically. It's not about being brilliant. It does take a certain intelligence, but mostly it's about instincts. You can take the smartest kid at Wharton, the one who gets straight A's and has a 170 IQ, and if he doesn't have the instincts, he'll never be a successful entrepreneur.

Moreover, most people who do have the instincts will never recognize that they do, because they don't have the courage or the good fortune to discover their potential. Somewhere out there are a few men with more innate talent at golf than Jack Nicklaus, or women with greater ability at tennis than Chris Evert or Martina Navratilova, but they will never lift a club or swing a racket and therefore will never find out how great they could have been. Instead, they'll be content to sit and watch stars perform on television.

When I look back at the deals I've made — and the ones I've lost or let pass — I see certain common elements. But unlike the real estate evangelists you see all over television these days, I can't promise you that by following the precepts I'm about to offer you'll become a millionaire overnight. Unfortunately, life rarely works that way, and most people who try to get rich quick end up going broke instead. As for those among you who do have the genes, who do have the instincts, and who could be highly successful, well, I still hope you won't follow my advice. Because that would just make it a much tougher world for me.

Think big

I like thinking big. I always have. To me it's very simple: if you're going to be thinking anyway, you might as well think big. Most people think small, because

116

most people are afraid of success, afraid of making decisions, afraid of winning. And that gives people like me a great advantage.

My father built low-income and middle-income buildings in Brooklyn and Queens, but even then, I gravitated to the best location. When I was working in Queens, I always wanted Forest Hills. And as I grew older, and perhaps wiser, I realized that Forest Hills was great, but Forest Hills isn't Fifth Avenue. And so I began to look toward Manhattan, because at a very early age, I had a true sense of what I wanted to do.

I wasn't satisfied just to earn a good living. I was looking to make a statement. I was out to build something monumental — something worth a big effort. Plenty of other people could buy and sell little brownstones, or build cookie-cutter red brick buildings. What attracted me was the challenge of building a spectacular development on almost one hundred acres by the river on the West Side of Manhattan, or creating a huge new hotel next to Grand Central Station at Park Avenue and 42nd Street.

The same sort of challenge is what attracted me to Atlantic City. It's nice to build a successful hotel. It's a lot better to build a hotel attached to a huge casino that can earn fifty times what you'd ever earn renting hotel rooms. You're talking a whole different order of magnitude.

One of the keys to thinking big is total focus. I think of it almost as a controlled neurosis, which is a quality I've noticed in many highly successful entrepreneurs. They're obsessive, they're driven, they're single-minded and sometimes they're almost maniacal, but it's all channeled into their work. Where other people are paralyzed by neurosis, the people I'm talking about are actually helped by it.

I don't say this trait leads to a happier life, or a better life, but it's great when it comes to getting what you want. This is particularly true in New York real estate, where you are dealing with some of the sharpest, toughest, and most vicious people in the world. I happen to love to go up against these guys, and I love to beat them.

Protect the Downside and the Upside Will Take Care of Itself

People think I'm a gambler. I've never gambled in my life. To me, a gambler is someone who plays slot machines. I prefer to own slot machines. It's a very good business being the house.

It's been said that I believe in the power of positive thinking. In fact, I believe in the power of negative thinking. I happen to be very conservative in business. I always go into the deal anticipating the worst. If you plan for the worst — if you can live with the worst, the good will always take care of itself. The only time in my life I didn't follow that rule was with the USFL. I bought a losing team in a losing league on a

117

long shot. It almost worked, through our antitrust suit, but when it didn't, I had no fallback. The point is that you can't be too greedy. If you go for a home run on every swing, you're also going to strike out a lot. I try never to leave myself too exposed, even if it means sometimes settling for a triple, a double, or even, on rare occasions, a single.

One of the best examples I can give is my experience in Atlantic City. Several years ago, I managed to piece together an incredible site on the Boardwalk. The individual deals I made for parcels were contingent on my being able to put together the whole site. Until I achieved that, I didn't have to put up very much money at all.

Once I assembled the site, I didn't rush to start construction. That meant I had to pay the carrying charges for a longer period, but before I spent hundreds of millions of dollars and several years on construction, I wanted to make sure I got my gaming license. I lost time, but I also kept my exposure much lower.

When I got my licensing on the Boardwalk site, Holiday Inns came along and offered to be my partner. Some people said, "You don't need them. Why give up fifty percent of your profits?" But Holiday Inns also offered to pay back the money I already had in the deal, to finance all the construction, and to guarantee me against losses for five years. My choice was whether to keep all the risk myself, and own 100 percent of the casino, or settle for a 50 percent stake without putting up a dime. It was an easy decision.

Barron Hilton, by contrast, took a bolder approach when he built his casino in Atlantic City. In order to get opened as quickly as possible, he filed for a license and began construction on a $400 million facility at the same time. But then, two months before the hotel was scheduled to open, Hilton was denied a license. He ended up selling to me at the last minute, under a lot of pressure, and without a lot of other options. I renamed the facility Trump's Castle and it is now one of the most successful hotel-casinos anywhere in the world.

Maximize your Options

I also protect myself by being flexible. I never get too attached to one deal or one approach. For starters, I keep a lot of balls in the air, because most deals fall out, no matter how promising they seem at first. In addition, once I've made a deal, I always come up with at least a half dozen approaches to making it work, because anything can happen, even to the best-laid plans.

For example, if I hadn't gotten the approvals I wanted for Trump Tower, I could always have built an office tower and done just fine. If I'd been turned down for licensing in Atlantic City, I could have sold the site I'd assembled to another casino operator, at a good profit. Perhaps the best example I can give is the first deal I made in Manhattan. I got an option to purchase the Penn Central rail yards at West

118

34th Street. My original proposal was to build middle-income housing on the site, with government financing. Unfortunately, the city began to have financial problems, and money for public housing suddenly dried up. I didn't spend a lot of time feeling sorry for myself. Instead, I switched to my second option and began promoting the site as ideal for a convention center. It took two years of pushing and promoting, but ultimately the city did designate my site for the convention center — and that's where it was built.

Of course, if they hadn't chosen my site, I would have come up with a third approach.

Know Your Market

Some people have a sense of the market and some people don't. Steven Spielberg has it. Lee Iacocca of Chrysler has it, and so does Judith Krantz in her way. Woody Allen has it, for the audience he cares about reaching, and so does Sylvester Stallone, at the other end of the spectrum. Some people criticize Stallone, but you've got to give him credit. I mean, here's a man who is just forty-one years old, and he's already created two of the all-time great characters, Rocky and Rambo. To me he's a diamond-in-the-rough type, a genius purely by instinct. He knows what the public wants and he delivers it.

I like to think I have that instinct. That's why I don't hire a lot of number-crunchers, and I don't trust fancy marketing surveys. I do my own surveys and draw my own conclusions. I'm a great believer in asking everyone for an opinion before I make a decision. It's a natural reflex. If I'm thinking of buying a piece of property, I'll ask the people who live nearby about the area — what they think of the schools and the crime and the shops. When I'm in another city and I take a cab, I'll always make it a point to ask the cabdriver questions. I ask and I ask and I ask, until I begin to get a gut feeling about something. And that's when I make a decision.

I have learned much more from conducting my own random surveys than I could ever have learned from the greatest of consulting firms. They send a crew of people down from Boston, rent a room in New York, and charge you $100,000 for a lengthy study. In the end, it has no conclusion, and takes so long to complete that if the deal you were considering was a good one, it will be long gone.

The other people I don't take too seriously are the critics — except when they stand in the way of my projects. In my opinion, they mostly write to impress each other, and they're just as swayed by fashions as anyone else. One week it's spare glass towers they are praising to the skies. The next week, they've rediscovered old, and they're celebrating detail and ornamentation. What very few of them have is any feeling for what the public wants. Which is why, if these critics ever tried to become developers, they'd be terrible failures. Trump Tower is a building the critics were skeptical about before it was built, but which the public obviously liked. I'm not talking about the sort of person who inherited money 175 years ago and lives on 84th Street and Park Avenue. I'm taking about the wealthy Italian with the beautiful wife and the red Ferrari. Those people — the audience I was after — came to Trump Tower in droves.

The funny thing about Trump Tower is that we ended up getting great architectural reviews. The critics didn't want to review it well because it stood for a lot of things they didn't like at the time. But in the end, it was such a gorgeous building that they had no choice but to say so. I always follow my own instincts, but I'm not going to kid you: it's also nice to get good reviews.

Use Your Leverage

The worst thing you can possibly do in a deal is seem desperate to make it. That makes the other guy smell blood, and then you're dead. The best thing you can do is deal from strength, and leverage is the biggest strength you can have. Leverage is having something the other guy wants. Or better yet, needs. Or best of all, simply can't do without.

Unfortunately, that isn't always the case, which is why leverage often requires imagination, and salesmanship. In other words, you have to convince the other guy it's in his interest to make the deal.

Back in 1974, in an effort to get the city to approve my deal to buy the Commodore Hotel on East 42nd Street, I convinced its owners to go public with the fact that they were planning to close down the hotel. After they made the announcement, I wasn't shy about pointing out to everyone in the city what a disaster a boarded-up hotel would be for the Grand Central area, and for the entire city.

When the board of Holiday Inns was considering whether to enter into a partnership with me in Atlantic City, they were attracted to my site because they believed my construction was farther along than that of any other potential partner. In reality, I wasn't that far along, but I did everything I could, short of going to work at the site myself, to assure them that my casino was practically finished. My leverage came from confirming an impression they were already predisposed to believe.

When I bought the West Side rail yards, I didn't name the project Television City by accident, and I didn't choose the name because I think it's pretty. I did it to make a point. Keeping the television networks in New York — and NBC in particular — is something the city very much wants to do. Losing a network to New Jersey would be a psychological and economic disaster.

Leverage: don't make deals without it.

Enhance Your Location

Perhaps the most misunderstood concept in all of real estate is that the key to success is location, location, location. Usually, that's said by people who don't know what they're talking about. First of all, you don't necessarily need the best location. What you need is the best deal. Just as you can create leverage, you can enhance a location, through promotion and through psychology.

When you have 57th Street and Fifth Avenue as your location, as I did with Trump Tower, you need less promotion. But even there, I took it a step further, by promoting Trump Tower as something almost larger than life. By contrast, Museum Tower, two blocks away and built above the Museum of Modem Art, wasn't marketed well, never achieved an "aura," and didn't command nearly the prices we did at Trump Tower.

Location also has a lot to do with fashion. You can take a mediocre location and turn it into something considerably better just by attracting the right people. After Trump Tower I built Trump Plaza, on a site at Third Avenue and 61st Street that I was able to purchase very inexpensively. The truth is that Third Avenue simply didn't compare with Fifth Avenue as a location. But Trump Tower had given a value to the Trump name, and I built a very striking building on Third Avenue. Suddenly we were able to command premium prices from very wealthy and successful people who might have chosen Trump Tower if the best apartments hadn't been sold out. Today Third Avenue is a very prestigious place to live, and Trump Plaza is a great success.

My point is that the real money isn't made in real estate by spending the top dollar to buy the best location. You can get killed doing that, just as you can get killed buying a bad location, even for a low price.

What you should never do is pay too much, even if that means walking away from a very good site. Which is all a more sophisticated way of looking at location.

Get the Word Out

You can have the most wonderful product in the world, but if people don't know about it, it's not going to be worth much. There are singers in the world with voices as good as Frank Sinatra's, but they're singing in their garages because no one has ever heard of them. You need to generate interest, and you need to create excitement. One way is to hire public relations people and pay them a lot of money to sell whatever you've got. But to me, that's like hiring outside consultants to study a market. It's never as good as doing it yourself.

One thing I've learned about the press is that they're always hungry for a good story, and the more sensational the better. It's the nature of the job, and I understand that. The point is that if you are a little different, or a little outrageous, or if you do things that are bold or controversial, the press is going to write about you. I've always done things a little differently, I don't mind controversy, and my deals tend to be somewhat ambitious. Also, I achieved a lot when I was very young, and I chose to live in a certain style. The result is that the press has always wanted to write about me. I'm not saying that they necessarily like me. Sometimes they write positively, and sometimes they write negatively. But from a pure business point of view, the benefits of being written about have far outweighed the drawbacks. It's really quite simple. If I take a full-page ad in the New York Times to publicize a project, it might cost $40,000, and in any case, people tend to be skeptical about advertising. But if the New York Times writes even a moderately positive one-column story about one of my deals, it doesn't cost me anything, and it's worth a lot more than $40,000.

The funny thing is that even a critical story, which may be hurtful personally, can be very valuable to your business. Television City is a perfect example. When I bought the land in 1985, many people, even those on the West Side, didn't realize that those one hundred acres existed. Then I announced I was going to build the world's tallest building on the site. Instantly, it became a media event: the New York Times put it on the front page, Dan Rather announced it on the evening news, and George Will wrote a column about it in Newsweek. Every architecture critic had an opinion, and so did a lot of editorial writers. Not all of them liked the idea of the world's tallest building. But the point is that we got a lot of attention, and that alone creates value.

The other thing I do when I talk with reporters is to be straight. I try not to deceive them or to be defensive, because those are precisely the ways most people get themselves into trouble with the press. Instead, when a reporter asks me a tough question, I try to frame a positive answer, even if that means shifting the ground. For example, if someone asks me what negative effects the world's tallest building might have on the West Side, I turn the tables and talk about how New Yorkers deserve the world's tallest building, and what a boost it will give the city to have that honor again. When a reporter asks why I build only for the rich, I note that the rich aren't the only ones who benefit from my buildings. I explain that I put thousands of people to work who might otherwise be collecting unemployment, and that I add to the city's tax base every time I build a new project. I also point out that buildings like Trump Tower have helped spark New York's renaissance.

The final key to the way I promote is bravado. I play to people's fantasies. People may not always think big themselves, but they can still get very excited by those who do. That's why a little hyperbole never hurts. People want to believe that something is the biggest and the greatest and the most spectacular. I call it truthful hyperbole. It's an innocent form of exaggeration — and a very effective form of promotion.

122

Fight Back

Much as it pays to emphasize the positive, there are times when the only choice is confrontation. In most cases I'm very easy to get along with. I'm very good to people who are good to me. But when people treat me badly or unfairly or try to take advantage of me, my general attitude, all my life, has been to fight back very hard. The risk is that you'll make a bad situation worse, and I certainly don't recommend this approach to everyone. But my experience is that if you're fighting for something you believe in — even if it means alienating some people along the way — things usually work out for the best in the end.

When the city unfairly denied me, on Trump Tower, the standard tax break every developer had been getting, I fought them in six different courts. It cost me a lot of money, I was considered highly likely to lose, and people told me it was a no-win situation politically. I would have considered it worth the effort regardless of the outcome. In this case, I won — which made it even better.

When Holiday Inns, once my partners at the Trump Plaza Hotel and Casino in Atlantic City, ran a casino that consistently performed among the bottom 50 percent of casinos in town, I fought them very hard and they finally sold out their share to me. Then I began to think about trying to take over the Holiday Inns company altogether.

Even if I never went on the offensive, there are a lot of people gunning for me now. One of the problems when you become successful is that jealousy and envy inevitably follow. There are people — I categorize them as life's losers — who get their sense of accomplishment and achievement from trying to stop others. As far as I'm concerned, if they had any real ability they wouldn't be fighting me, they'd be doing something constructive themselves.

Deliver the Goods

You can't con people, at least not for long. You can create excitement, you can do wonderful promotion and get all kinds of press, and you can throw in a little hyperbole. But if you don't deliver the goods, people will eventually catch on.

I think of Jimmy Carter. After he lost the election to Ronald Reagan, Carter came to see me in my office. He told me he was seeking contributions to the Jimmy Carter Library. I asked how much he had in mind. And he said, "Donald, I would be very appreciative if you contributed five million dollars."

I was dumbfounded. I didn't even answer him.

But that experience also taught me something. Until then, I'd never understood how Jimmy Carter became president. The answer is that as poorly qualified as he was for the job, Jimmy Carter had the nerve, the guts, the balls, to ask for something extraordinary. That ability above all helped him get elected president. But then, of course, the American people caught on pretty quickly that Carter couldn't do the job, and he lost in a landslide when he ran for reelection.

I see the same thing in my business, which is full of people who talk a good game but don't deliver. When Trump Tower became successful, a lot of developers got the idea of imitating our atrium, and they ordered their architects to come up with a design. The drawings would come back, and they would start costing out the job.

What they discovered is that the bronze escalators were going to cost a million dollars extra, and the waterfall was going to cost two million dollars, and the marble was going to cost many millions more. They saw that it all added up to many millions of dollars, and all of a sudden these people with these great ambitions would decide, well, let's forget about the atrium.

The dollar always talks in the end. I'm lucky, because I work in a very, very special niche, at the top of the market, and I can afford to spend top dollar to build the best. I promoted the hell out of Trump Tower, but I also had a great product to promote.

Contain the Costs

I believe in spending what you have to. But I also believe in not spending more than you should. When I was building low-income housing, the most important thing was to get it built quickly, inexpensively, and adequately, so you could rent it out and make a few bucks. That's when I learned to be cost-conscious. I never threw money around. I learned from my father that every penny counts, because before too long your pennies turn into dollars.

To this day, if I feel a contractor is overcharging me, I'll pick up the phone, even if it's only for $5,000 or $10,000, and I'll complain. People say to me, "What are you bothering for, over a few bucks?" My answer is that the day I can't pick up the telephone and make a twenty-five-cent call to save $10,000 is the day I'm going to close up shop.

The point is that you can dream great dreams, but they'll never amount to much if you can't turn them into reality at a reasonable cost. At the time I built Trump Plaza in Atlantic City, banks were reluctant to finance new construction at all, because almost every casino up to then had experienced tens of millions of dollars in cost overruns. We brought Trump Plaza in on budget, and on time. As a result, we were able to open for Memorial Day weekend, the start of the high season. By contrast, Bob Guccione of Penthouse has been trying for the past seven years to build a casino on the Boardwalk site right next to ours. All he has to show for his efforts is a rusting half-built frame and tens of millions of dollars in lost revenues and squandered carrying costs.

www.mentorsmagazine.com

Even small jobs can get out of control if you're not attentive. For nearly seven years I watched from the window of my office as the city tried to rebuild Wollman Rink in Central Park. At the end of that time, millions of dollars had been wasted and the job was farther from being completed than when the work began. They were all set to rip out the concrete and start over when I finally couldn't stand it anymore, and I offered to do it myself. The job took four months to complete at a fraction of the city's cost.

Have Fun

I don't kid myself. Life is very fragile, and success doesn't change that. If anything, success makes it more fragile. Anything can change, without warning, and that's why I try not to take any of what's happened too seriously. Money was never a big motivation for me, except as a way to keep score. The real excitement is playing the game. I don't spend a lot of time worrying about what I should have done differently, or what's going to happen next. If you ask me exactly what the deals I'm about to describe all add up to in the end, I'm not sure I have a very good answer. Except that I've had a very good time making them.

Donald Trump is a billionaire real estate developer who has amassed a fortune through owning key New York properties, and Atlantic City casinos. He has gained fame for his flamboyant deals and lavish lifestyle. He is the author of four books and most recently an immensely popular TV show.

Article reprint from Trump, The Art Of The Deal *©1987.*
Printed here by permission.

Brave New World
of Real Estate Investing

by Stephen E. Roulac

Should you, as a real estate investor, stay close to home? Or, should you venture to far away lands?

Should you invest only in your backyard, in properties that are close to where you live? Or should you venture to distant shores to invest internationally? Can you picture yourself doing that?

Do you like to travel to foreign places? Do you like to invest in real estate? Would you like to combine the two? International real estate investing may be just the ticket to a globetrotter lifestyle that you may have dreamed about but — until now — never thought possible.

The fact is that you can invest internationally without ever leaving home. Or, you can travel throughout the world, searching for, acquiring, and managing exciting foreign real estate investments. If you want to enhance your local real estate investing, then you should consider international real estate investing.

Until very recently, international real estate investing was not practical for all but the most substantial, sophisticated and worldly of entrepreneurs. But the advent of global property securities — enabling investors to buy and sell shares of property enterprises throughout the world, just as they can buy and sell company stocks — has transformed the real estate investing landscape. Reviewing the startling discoveries two entrepreneurs whose ideas changed real estate forever can provide a provocative context for appreciating the profoundly revolutionary implications of investing in real estate through owning shares of property enterprises.

New Horizons

More than a half millennium ago, Christopher Columbus challenged the conventional thinking that the world was flat. Though some recognized that far away lands offered riches and opportunity, few were willing to embark upon a journey to the unknown. Most favored the nearby, the familiar, the safe. But Christopher

Columbus decided to go further in the pursuit of his courageous conviction that opportunity awaited. His explorations opened up new horizons in trade, creating new jobs and new opportunities beyond anyone's perception or dreams.

Shortly after Columbus sailed from Western Europe in 1492 in search of a brave new world, Nicholas Copernicus in 1514 proposed the radical idea that the sun, not the earth, was the center of the universe. According to Copernicus's highly controversial theory, the planets and the stars, including the earth and its moon, orbit the sun. This radical idea was banned by many countries, because it contradicted the powerful Catholic Church's view of the earth as the center of the universe. This endorsed view had been articulated in the second century by the Egyptian astronomer Ptolemy, who advanced the theory that each planet orbited in an elliptical or circular path around the earth, which was assumed to be the center of the universe.

Even though Christopher Columbus set foot on the North American shore, rather than India as he mistakenly perceived, his courageous exploration triggered phenomenal subsequent consequences. And though Copernicus did not have all of the details exactly worked out, his theory was the basis for challenging Ptolemy's earth-centered view. This challenge introduced a dramatically new way to view nature, society, and ultimately commerce.

Columbus and Copernicus advanced ideas that challenged the very core of the philosophic foundations and political power structures of society. Similarly, real estate investing has long rested on the foundation of *close to home*. Although there are very good reasons that real estate investors favor investing close to home, forward-looking, ambitious entrepreneurs and investors increasingly recognize that there is a brave new world of opportunity in far away places.

At-Home Investing

Although professional real estate investment books discuss the concept of portfolio diversification — including investing in properties in different places — such discussions are primarily oriented to institutional investors, rather than individual investors. Additionally, although a few real estate investing gurus, systems and courses explore going to different places in search of real estate opportunities, a majority emphasize investing in their local hometown.

As appealing as the opportunities may, or may not, be in your hometown, you will recognize that there are many more opportunities *outside* than in your hometown. For example, each of the 3,425 metropolises throughout the world with a population over 100,000 contain scores of thousands of real estate investment opportunities. Some of the very largest metropolises contain millions of real estate investment opportunities!

International Investing Appeal

If you were to invest internationally, you could take advantage of many more opportunities than you could ever encounter in your hometown. And, apart from the magnitude of those numerous opportunities — and the basic compelling reasons to invest in local real estate — the rationale for investing in international real estate includes a number of other persuasive reasons, such as:

- Participating in the awesome expansion of places that are growing much faster
- Converting your travel, knowledge, intellectual, relationship, or curiosity interests in other countries, people and places into a sound investing program
- Transferring your particular professional and amateur insights, ideas, possibilities, and areas of expertise to other places, where you may have a competitive advantage over others who don't know, or can't do, as much as you
- Bringing a fresh eyes perspective to new places — seeing opportunities that others who are so close to the situation do not perceive
- Solving the problem of what to do in regard to real estate investing when your place is suffering an economic downturn
- Catching and riding the wave of growth and expansion in other places
- Enjoying legitimate business reasons to travel to other places to research and check in on your investments
- Engaging in global diversification, so you are not depending exclusively on the United States political and economic system, but are spreading your real estate investing involvements throughout different places

By investing internationally, you may not only make higher investment returns, but also realize these benefits that are not available through local real estate investment.

Barriers to International Investing

As appealing as international investing is, most investors face major barriers in investing beyond their hometown, including:

- Time and cost of travel to evaluate investing opportunities
- Difficulty in managing distant properties
- Lack of foreign language fluency
- Lack of local culture knowledge
- Lack of knowledge of local laws and regulations
- Lack of knowledge of local legal ownership forms
- Lack of knowledge of local leasing practice
- Lack of knowledge of local property management practices
- Lack of connections with local professional service providers
- Lack of connections with property maintenance and construction resources
- Few or no contacts with local business leaders
- Lack of knowledge of local political processes

- Lack of connections and access to politicians and government officials
- Lack of knowledge of different economies
- Lack of familiarity with local economy
- Lack of knowledge of local currency
- Risks of currency fluctuations
- Difficulty achieving diversification with small scale money to invest
- Overwhelming amount of information to understand and evaluate
- Lack of tools and techniques to compare investing in different places

These are all discouragements to international real estate investing. But, when you think about it, problems and difficulties that the individual investor faces in participating in international real estate are not that different from those investors face in different types of corporate business entities. If the business has shares you can buy, investing in real estate in a foreign country is not that much different than investing in a business.

Securitization Overcomes the Problems

The advent of *securitization* — making available *a share* of the business, and thereby replacing the necessity for the investor to own and operate the entire business — has not only transformed companies' ability to get access to capital, it has also transformed investors' ability to get access to desired investment opportunities.

And today the same positive advantages that apply in securitization for corporations also apply in securitization for real estate. *Real estate securitization* makes available the multiple advantages of common stock ownership. The advance of real estate securitization allows an investor to assemble a diverse portfolio of interests in real estate enterprises in a manner very similar to investors participating in the stock market.

Advances in real estate securitization have changed the investment landscape. Just as corporate securities allow investors to participate on a smaller scale than buying an entire business, so too do real estate securities enable investors to buy shares in enterprises that own portfolios of properties, rather than having to buy entire buildings.

For the vast majority of investors, the arguments favoring investing via property securities are irrefutable. Property securities should represent the core component of most investor's real estate investing program. While for some investors, a direct investing program supplementing the securities investing program may be warranted, for most investors, property securities are the only efficient, effective and feasible way to invest generally — especially internationally.

Mogul Lifestyle

In addition to the less dramatic aspects of investing in international real estate stocks, doing so can also enable you to live the mogul lifestyle. Do you think Donald Trump does all of the work in managing properties himself? No. To get the results he wants, Trump ties people's pay to their performance. He has others do the work for him. If he doesn't like how they perform, he fires them.

By investing in international real estate securities, you can live the mogul lifestyle and manage your real estate investment activities in ways similar to the way Donald Trump manages his real estate empire. When you invest in an international real estate stock, you'll recognize how much extraordinary work has been done for you, even before you invest.

The more you learn about international real estate investing, the more you may find it to your liking. International real estate investing provides phenomenal new experiences. Consider that the costs associated with the investment are legitimate and appropriate expenses for managing your investments. Legitimate and appropriate expenses, of course, are deductible for tax purposes.

Because international real estate investing allows you to avoid lots of the burdens, aggravations, problems and hard work of direct local real estate investing, it is possible to invest in international real estate without ever leaving the privacy of your study, the comfort of your living room couch, or the convenience of your kitchen table.

How You Can Benefit from International Real Estate Investing

By being an international real estate investor, you benefit by:

- Living the Donald Trump mogul lifestyle
- Traveling to new, exciting and fun places
- Converting a non-deductible personal expense into a legitimate business expense
- Making your dollars go farther by patronizing businesses that you already own — property investment companies, hotels, retailers — when you travel
- Spending less time on your international real estate investing than on your local real estate investing
- Capitalizing on your insights into global politics and economics through actual investment opportunities
- Connecting with growth opportunities in the "old country" by making investments there
- Being a player in the international real estate markets, on the same terms as the best and brightest, while being relieved of the management burdens.

An international real estate investor participates in growth around the world: More people in a place means more demand for property, which leads to higher potential property values in that place. And, if the people living, working, playing, visiting, and doing business in the place have higher incomes, are spending more and investing more, this leads to higher realized property values. Population growth and prosperity are the twin engines of successful international real estate investing.

Key ingredients of the *magic appeal of international real estate* include:

- Faster results — You can get to work and build an international real estate portfolio much faster then you might imagine
- Easier — Much less effort is required than for local real estate
- Greater benefit for effort — For the same amount of money invested in direct real estate, you can own much more international real estate. For the same amount of time expended to buy a single piece of hometown real estate, you can buy a whole portfolio of international real estate.
- Partner with the shrewdest, savviest property entrepreneurs in the world, investing alongside them on the very same terms that they invested
- Get Rich While You Sleep

Investing only in your own backyard real estate is somewhat akin to insisting that (1) the world is flat and that (2) the sun and all planets and stars in the galaxy rotate around the earth. For many, that thinking serves them well. But for those who aspire to venture into the Brave New World to discover distant lands and expand their horizons, international real estate investing offers extraordinary opportunities and rich rewards.

Stephen Roulac is the CEO of Roulac Global Places LLC, and is the world's leading authority on the economic productivity and strategic importance of the places in which we live and work. He is known for his ability to achieve extraordinary outcomes for his clients. He was named Millennium Real Estate Award Honoree by U. C. Berkeley, recognizing those individuals who have had the greatest impact upon the real estate industry in the 20th century. Call 1-888-765-18295, fax 415-451-4343, or email experts@roulacglobalplaces.com to request your free report, "How You Can Create Your Winning Real Estate Strategy." You can also learn more by going to www.roulacglobalplaces.com.

Money Has No Power of its Own

by Suze Orman

When I first started writing about money and talking about it on television, my mother was horrified. I wrote about my mom and dad, and the hard times we experienced financially when I was growing up. I wrote about the many times I messed up with money myself as I was finding my way as an adult. My mom would say, Suze, I have spent my whole life hiding the truth from everyone and now you go on TV and tell the whole world.

In time, however, she stopped being upset with me, and even came to approve of what I was doing. People who ran into her would thank her for letting me tell the truth about our situation, because it had been their situation too, and their neighbors and friends situation. Few people talk openly about their finances or tell one another the same things they say behind closed doors. My mom learned that telling the truth about money can be liberating.

Today my mom is eighty-nine. She and I now spend more time talking about the years that she may or may not have left than we talk about money. Just a few months ago, I asked her during one of these conversations, "What is the most surprising thing that you have learned in your life?" Her answer shocked me. She said that finally, after all these years, she had come to realize that she was more powerful than her money. When I asked her what she meant by that, this is what she said.

Suze's Mom's Lesson:
True power does not reside in a bank account

Suze, even though it is getting harder for me to live alone, at this point I can still cook for myself and for you and your brothers, I can drive myself to the grocery store to get what I need whenever I need it. And that, my dear Suze, is more than almost all my friends can do at this point in their lives — regardless of how much money they have. When your father died, I thought my biggest problem was going to be that I didn't have enough money to be okay for the rest of my life. Remember? That was before you had any money. Because I thought I didn't have money, I felt powerless. I'd inherited this condo and a small sum of money, but even so I had no idea what to do with them. Little by little, though, with your help, I learned how to make ends meet and work with what I had so that I could create what I now have today. So, today I do have enough. In fact, I have more than enough. But the money, to my surprise, is not what is making me feel powerful. Don't get me wrong. Thank goodness I have it. It gives me great peace of mind to know that I can pay my bills, go to visit my sister in Florida, and go out to eat whenever I want.

However, all the money in the world would not be enough to enable me to do all that I do at my age on my own. I look at my friends, the few who are still alive, and now my greatest fear is that one day I will end up in a nursing home like many of them and not have the power to take care of myself Money is not the solution to that problem for me, and that surprises me.

My mom is right.

Money is definitely a vital force in your life, but as my mom was saying, it is not your life force. Where many people tend to go wrong is that they somehow think, just as my mom did years ago, that money will make them powerful. I can t tell you the number of times I ye been talking to someone who is in serious financial trouble and all of a sudden she looks up to the heavens and says, God, I wish I had some more money. Money is never a permanent solution to any problem. Money can come in to your life but it can also go out. Look at all the people who have won millions in the lotteries — many of them have less today than they did even before they won.

You already know that wishing or praying for more money will not solve your problems, or you wouldn't be reading this book. Nonetheless, I want you to redefine money for yourself. Many people define their own self-worth by how much money they have. But it's you who give your money its energy, force, and direction. You give it potential, meaning, and life. When you do, your actions with money enable you to keep what you have and create what you deserve in your life.

I know this truth can be difficult to accept, because the world we live in does seem to define everything according to monetary standards. But this law was really brought home to me in another way.

Suze's Lessons:
A penny lost is a lesson learned

One hot summer day in New York City, I was taking my favorite walk along Third Avenue, past all the wonderful stores with their window displays offering everything under the sun — fancy furniture in one store and simple trinkets in the next. Summer is my favorite time of the year in New York, and I took this same walk every day, crossing Third Avenue at Fifty-ninth Street and continuing up the avenue past Bloomingdale s. I had turned this walk into a daily ritual, one that I loved.

133

An integral part of my ritual was bending down in the middle of Fifty-ninth and Third to try to retrieve two pennies that were embedded deep in the tar in the middle of that well-trafficked intersection. Both these pennies had been there for as long as I could remember. I usually used my bare hands to try to pry those pennies out (no tools allowed in my game), and more than once I drew smiles or puzzled looks from others crossing the street. My efforts were tied to the timing of the lights, and my little game ended each day when I had to stop to let the traffic move on. This had become quite an obsession with me. I remained convinced that one day I would set free at least one of those pennies.

On this particular day — the hottest I can remember in New York City, so hot in fact that steam was rising from the sidewalks — I was passing my penny pit, as I called it. I bent down, dug in a nail, and pulled on one of the pennies. The tar was soft, softer than it had ever been, and it seemed to me that the penny moved — for the first time ever. I continued digging and pulling on this one penny, ignoring the fact that I was utterly destroying my thirteen-dollar manicure. I could feel the penny moving, the tar yielding. With one more tug, to my amazement, it came up. I have to tell you, I felt as if I had just won the lottery. I was jubilant. I had set that penny free. I tried for a second to get the other one out, but the light was changing, the traffic was threatening, and I decided to let the other penny alone. I was as happy as I could be with my accomplishment.

And then this is what happened. While I was waiting at the next corner for the traffic light to change again, I started to flip this penny, throwing it in the air and having just a great time with it. I was already thinking, "What will I do with this penny that I ye been trying to get for years, now that I finally have it?" At that moment, I accidentally dropped the penny. I watched as the penny — moving as if in slow motion — landed on its side, rolled a few inches, and went right down into the drainage grate. Gone! I could not believe it. It was like a bad joke. It had taken years to get that penny, and just a few minutes to lose it.

Money has no power of its own

This little adventure with a penny was a graphic lesson for me and a new way of looking at money. With my own eyes, I saw how money — or in this case, a penny was unable to do anything on its own. The penny had been totally inert and would have stayed right where it was, forever and a day (just like the other penny, which is still there) until some other nut took a serious amount of time to pry it out of that tar and spend it, save it, or lose it, as I did.

What happens to that penny, or any penny, depends completely on a person's actions. Do you see that money has no power of its own? All its power flows through you. People first, then money.

As a group, the first four laws create a road map to help you take control of your money both financially and emotionally. Law 5 focuses even more on your inner power than Law 3 (Do what is right for you before you do what is right for your money). It's one thing to know what is right for you and your money and another to have the power to act on that knowledge.

So to personalize this law for you, please ask yourself these questions. If you have been taking actions with your money, and you still don t feel powerful in your life, why don t you? And if you have been using money as a substitute for power, why is that?

Suze Orman is a Certified Financial Planner professional and a best-selling author of personal finance books, lecturer, host of both radio and television shows.

To book a speaking engagement with Suze contact:
International Creative Management
Lecture Division
Carol Bruckner
email: cbruckner@icrntalent.com
212.556.5602

Suze's Agent is: Amanda Urban
International Creative Management
212.556.5600

Probate

Making it BIG in Probate

by George Miller

I started my Real Estate investing training in 1984. Yes, you guessed it, I heard about it through one of those TV commercials that you see on late night television. I was living in upstate New York in a small apartment that I couldn't afford with my construction laborer salary. I remember how desperate I was to make a change. I heard testimonials of people making $10,000–$50,000 or more on a single real estate deal. I had just been laid off for the winter without enough employed weeks to collect unemployment for a long cold New York State winter. Up against a wall, I took my last $395 and mailed it off to this TV real estate guru. I called my landlord and let her know that I would not be paying the rent that month because I had just spent it on a get rich quick seminar. She was upset, to say the least.

A couple of weeks later I was sitting in a hotel 65 miles from my apartment, completely excited over what was about to unfold. It was an amazing weekend and the beginning of my real estate investing career. They talked about wraparound mortgages and reverse amortizing loans — a whole new language I never heard before. I didn't get all the techniques, but what I did get was the sense that this was for me. I was finally really excited to be alive. I was excited about the possibilities the future held in store for me. I was on my way.

I've never forgotten what it took to make that first move. I had to have the courage to bet it all on me, a guy that only had one real possession: belief in himself. The reason I tell you this story isn't to impress you with what I have accomplished in my life, but to encourage you to take action for your life.

Over the past twenty years I have learned the value of these kinds of seminars. I have attended and bought just about every real estate course available. I am constantly a student of this great industry of Real Estate investment. My library is full with subject matters like Foreclosure, Pre-Foreclosure, Tax Deed Sales, No Money Down, Bankruptcy and on and on. I have spent my life in educating myself on how to make the big money and finding the next colossal opportunity. Hands down, I believe probate to be just that.

Today, I bring you one of real estate's best kept secrets: PROBATE! If you want to make the Big Money in real estate you will want to explore this exciting field. It is truly one of the most rewarding sectors of the real estate investment industry. Not only can you make loads of money, you get to help people who really want and need your help. The best part is you can do all of this without the use of your own money. Yes, you read right! You do not have to have a fat wallet in order to do this amazing business. If you are willing to take action for your life, you can make big money with probate. You will have to be able to read and write and have the desire to have a new possibility show up in your life. If you possess these three abilities, read on!

Making Big Money in the Probate Business

The first thing you need to do is invest in yourself. Get the best education you can find. Read and read it again. Be a human sponge for information. I have done just that. I have researched and spent an enormous amount of time and money in uncovering the secrets of probate. Then, you must apply what you learn to real life. Apply knowledge (book smarts) to practical situations. Notice what works and what doesn't. Adjust what doesn't work and improve and innovate what does work. That's it – that's the secret to making big money in probate.

After bagging a few estate deals that landed me some big checks, I gained a serious interest in this real estate niche. I looked at what my average profit was on the run of the mill real estate deal and what the average check was for probate or estates. I was excited! I looked at what was working and I began to innovate what was already working. It happened by accident at first. I occasionally came across these deals as a matter of course in my everyday marketing. I started paying attention to how I gained these new and profitable clients. Then I set out to find a system to flush out these kinds of clients in a predictable and systemized manner. I bought books, did internet research, sought out experts in the field, and went to the courthouse and asked for a list of probate filings. All this still didn't work as well as I wanted it to, so we created a system that does. I was amazed that there wasn't very much information available on probate investing or that the information was not very systemized. So I set out to get this Big Money system underway.

One of the hard cold facts I discovered is that we are all going to die. I know, I don't like it either…but it will happen. When it does we will pass our belongings on to our loved ones, friends, charities or even our pets. Sometimes, we leave one item or several items to a group of people. This item may or may not be wanted in its present form. Heirs may want to convert it to cash, which can be divided much better than concrete blocks or wood. So, they wait to see how the executor or personal representative of the will wants to dispose of the assets. Unfortunately, the executor probably didn't have much experience when he accepted this position. Executors typically do not know how to be a great executor or personal representative. They get some advice from the attorney and wing the rest.

137

Imagine that there is a way to systematically get your message to these executors. Your message is one of understanding and help. You see, most times the executor and the heirs just want the probate to be over as soon as possible. Generally that means paying the descendants' creditors, and in order to that you must either have cash in the estate or you must raise cash. Unfortunately — or fortunately — most estates don't have an abundance of cash in it. Either the heirs must come up with money themselves or they must sell the assets to settle the estate. In my experience, the heirs do not want to give up their weekly paycheck to fund the probate so it seems sensible to liquidate some or all of the assets of the estate. That's where we get to serve our clients.

The Truth about Probate

At first glance it may seem we are ambulance chasers, but we are the furthest from it. We are truly providing a service to people who really want our help. The person may be going through a trying time and just wants someone they can trust to handle the liquidation of the estate in the simplest and most convenient manner possible. Estates can contain everything under the sun: jewelry, stocks, bonds, cars, furniture, real estate. You may be required to handle all of these transactions.

Generally, when you even hear the word estate or probate you probably hear a DEAL. When you read "Estate Sale" in the paper or on a road sign your mind goes to "there must be a deal." That is because there usually is. Over the years people have been known to give away deals when liquidating an estate and you have been conditioned to think that way as well, with just cause. There is enormous money to be made in Probate.

Here is one example of a testimonial letter from a smart investor reaping the rewards from probate and estate investing.

Dear George,

After working with you for years, I still never cease to be amazed at the insights you continually come up with. With the information that you have given me on estates and probates, I see a new revenue stream coming my way in a realm that I had no real idea how to tap into, yet always knew was worth tapping into. In layman's terms, your material is easy to follow and understand, and I say anybody who can follow your simple system will succeed! Best wishes for continued success!!!

— Josh, We Buy Houses Cash

There are multitudes of ways to make huge profits in probate or estates – real estate liquidation and personal property (cars, jewelry, boats, planes, recreational vehicles, antiques), discounted mortgage liquidation, and buying creditors' positions at big discounts, knowing you're going to be paid because the assets far outweigh the debt. There are so many ways to make huge profits in probate that there may not be enough room to list them all! They are only limited by your imagination.

Whether you are a beginning investor or a seasoned professional, you will want to add these real estate secrets to your arsenal and blow the roof off the house with big profits. We have an easy-to-follow course which will walk you through the probate process from start to finish in a simple, easy to understand format for your listing. There is a document CD with every marketing letter you could want to generate clients for your probate machine, as well as all the documents you will need to put the deal together.

Gaining the Advantage

With more and more people realizing that real estate is a great way of kicking dreams into overdrive, you will need to keep on the cutting edge of real estate investing to be competitive. Once you have bought this educational course you will have an unfair advantage over your competition. These closely held secrets are now available to you to produce huge profits for you and your family. Don't you owe it to yourself to find out how to have a life that others have achieved through knowing these secrets? Can't you see yourself cashing those big checks, too? It all starts with getting the best education available and then putting your best asset to work…and that's you!

I'm not going to kid you. If you think that all you have to do is read a book and listen to a couple of CD's to make huge profits, this course isn't for you. But if you are willing to mix some great knowledge with a lot of "get out and do it," you too can realize huge profits with these best kept secrets. You can do what everyone else does and get similar results, or you can take advantage of cutting edge information and get extraordinary results for your life.

I personally challenge you to get the information you need to make huge profits and to live your dreams. Invest in your knowledge and get into action now. You too can realize what so many have already discovered in the secrets of probate and estate investing. Listen, I know you may feel a little uncertain. I too have felt that same feeling. But what I have found is that if I am willing to invest in myself, I can reap the rewards for a lifetime. A good friend of mine once told me "at the end you will either have everything that you want or excuses of why you don't have it." Which will you have?

I can't wait to meet you at one of our events. See you at the top!

George Miller is a brilliant Real Estate Investor and one of the nations most sought after speakers. George started his real estate training in 1984 and since then he has created an amazing reputation in just about every real-estate niche known to man. He is currently opening We Buy Houses Cash ™ *offices across the country and is committed to integrity as a backbone to his ventures.*

One of George's many talents is creating gigantic checks through Probated Properties. These hidden secrets are known only by a few select investors and they are now available through George's speaking engagements, weekend intensives, and home study courses. The information contained in these events is truly cutting edge information that could create a devastating advantage over other investors.

Call George's offices to find out how you can get this amazing technology through his speaking engagements, easy to follow home study courses or the weekend intensives that are jam packed with cutting edge information. His office number is (727) 548-HOME or email SM1@WeBuyHousesCash.com.

140

Section II

Surprise Bonus Section

Rare personal interview with Ron LeGrand!

RON LeGRAND

Ron LeGrand
Millionaire Maker

Interviewed by Linda Forsythe

Today I'm honored to interview Ron LeGrand, who is one of the most renowned and respected Real Estate Investors in the U.S! Ron LeGrand had to borrow money to attend his first real estate seminar 20 years ago when he was bankrupt and running a gas station. Today, he is recognized as the nation's leading authority on buying and selling single-family homes for fast cash with no credit and little or no personal investment or risk. He has personally "quick-turned" hundreds of houses and continues to actively pursue real estate deals to this day.

Author, trainer, lecturer, consultant and entrepreneur extraordinaire, Ron has earned a reputation as the best in his field. His one-day workshops are routinely standing-room-only and his boot camps continue to grow in popularity. Ron's secret is simple: his programs work — as evidenced by the thousands of successful real estate entrepreneurs all across North America who call him by the affectionate title, "The Guru."

Let's begin our interview …

Linda: *Ron, talk to us about how you first got started. Tell us about your early days.*

Ron: Well, that was back in 1982 when I was working on cars for a living, Linda. I used to be a mechanic. I was 35 years old before I learned how to spell real estate! I was dead broke, bankrupt, lost and I didn't know what I wanted to be when I grew up — but I knew it wasn't fixing cars all day in the hot Florida sun. I received an opportunity to attend a real estate seminar. The plan was to learn how to buy houses with nothing down and get rich by next Thursday. Since it didn't cost me anything to check it out … that's exactly what I did. I went down and the gentleman said, "If you can come up with $450 and attend my seminar next weekend … I will teach you all about real estate."

That excited me somewhat, but I had a little problem. Actually, I had 450 little problems. I didn't have the money so I had to borrow it. That gave me my start although I didn't learn a whole lot in that seminar. I was brand new and had no background in real estate but I did pick up a couple of techniques that inspired me. Within the first three weeks after being turned loose, I went out and received my first check for $3,000.

That turned my life around. I immediately called my boss and quit. I haven't been back since. But I went out and started buying all the wrong kind of properties in the wrong kind of areas for the wrong kind of reasons ... just because I could. Before you knew it, a couple of years had passed and, gosh, I had amassed over $1,000,000 in equity! I was a millionaire — on paper. I acquired 276 units during that time. 276 tenants — actually, 276 grandchildren looking for me to solve all their petty problems. I suddenly realized that this empire I had built was going to come crashing down around my neck if something didn't change. My income was beginning to be exceeded by my outgo in a series of vacancies. All I did was create a mess.

It took me FIVE years to sell off that mess and get my sanity back. I was seven years into the business before I finally realized what it was all about. There were no systems back then; there was no one to take me by the hand and lead me into the real estate world, so I had to figure it all out on my own. During that time I created systems for buying and selling single-family houses without using credit or money, and over the years created a huge number of millionaires by teaching those systems.

I guess what probably makes me the best of the best is that my students come back and teach me what they learn. I incorporate it and we stay right on the cutting edge, because I am actively involved in the business — I actually do this stuff. I guess that makes me kind of a weird teacher. My secretary (actually my former secretary Donna), is now my business partner. I buy several houses per month here in Jacksonville, Florida where I live. My total involvement in the business is about an hour a week talking to her. She spends 10 to 15 hours a week doing the business because of the systems I taught her. Our net profit is about $40,000 per transaction. What's even better, it's really a part-time business, but it produces a massive full-time income.

Linda: *Amazing! Ron, what was your belief when you first got started? I understand you went to that first seminar and became excited about the real estate business. But what was your belief BEFORE that?*

Ron: Well, before I went to that seminar I had the same skepticism most people have — and justifiably so. There's an awful lot of crap out there in the world nowadays. I believed it wouldn't apply to me because I didn't have any money and I didn't have any credit anyway. It didn't take me long to figure out that wasn't true. In fact, there are two ways to lose in my business, Linda.

Number one: if you write a big check to buy a house, you can always lose that big check. Don't write big check, can't lose big check — it's not rocket science. So, we don't write big checks to buy houses. Number two: we don't jeopardize our credit. The last thing I want anybody to do is go down to the bank and get a loan to buy a house. That is not the way you create wealth; that's the way you create bankruptcy and insanity. We buy properties without using our credit and without jeopardizing our money. And in addition, we are very careful not to make promises we can't keep. I didn't know these two important points back then. I didn't know there was a whole world of real estate out there you could work in without doing things the way the non-educated people think it ought to be done. I just assumed it wouldn't work for me. It didn't take me long to figure that out. It took me three weeks to get my first check and that was the beginning for me.

Linda: *If you could think back, what was that turning point that elevated your success?*

Ron: Well, my turning point was actually making the conscious decision to attend that seminar. It would have been a lot easier not to go; I had a lot of things to do. I was only half into it mentally. I just assumed it was a bunch of junk but something compelled me to go. But more importantly, I guess, what makes me different from a lot of folks out there that attend seminars nowadays is that I actually went home and started using the information.

The tools I learned I started implementing — just one or two things — and I got my first check. That built my confidence up enough to know there was no turning back. I really did quit my job three weeks into the business. I quickly got another check, and another, and another and pretty soon confidence sure wasn't the issue because I was out there buying houses like a madman. Once I actually convinced myself it could be done, there was no stopping me. I guess it all comes down to a commitment level. I was just committed. See, I knew I could always go get another job — but I also knew real estate could make me filthy stinking rich if I just stuck with it.

Linda: *Could anybody who's reading this interview become a successful real estate investor?*

Ron: Well, anybody who is willing to pay the price and invest the time and commitment that it takes to learn the ropes. I don't want to lead anybody to believe there's any magic pill here. There's no magic wand that I can wave over someone. It's going to take a little education process and you've got to be able to go through that. Unfortunately the same thing applies to any business, no matter what it is. There's no business worth doing that doesn't have the same process. It's a requirement. It's not a request; it's a requirement.

You've got to learn the basics, and then you've got to implement the basics. Make mistakes, screw up and go make some more mistakes, screw up and pretty soon you look back and you can't believe how smart you are.

Linda: *Ron, what do you love about real estate?*

Ron: Well, there are all kinds of benefits to it, and quite a few of them you can't find in other businesses. One of the biggest is you can start immediately — without money, without credit — and create some huge incomes very, very quickly. You know, I can't tell you how many times I see people create more revenue in a few months after starting than they did in their entire job, swapping hours for dollars working for someone else, walking over the dollars to get to the dimes. That's one of the best things I like about it, the ability to make big money quickly.

I like a lot of things about real estate. It'll never run out on us. It works every single place in the country where there are people who live and I don't care what the market is; up, down, sideways, it makes no difference. People always have to have shelter, Linda. They have to have a place to live.

When I started in 1982 the prime rate was 18%. Today it is way down in the single digits. I was making a bunch of money back then and I'm making a bunch of money today in real estate because I've learned people have to have shelter. Once you have the ability to help sellers out of the property and get buyers into the property without risking your money or credit, or making promises you can't keep, there's just a never-ending supply of deals out there for you.

Did you know that right now as we speak it has never been easier to do deals in real estate? All the ingredients are there. It's just one of those magic times. You've got foreclosures at a 52-year high, interest rates at a 60-year low and a glut of money out there chasing deals. The fact is, I call it the perfect storm. It's just a perfect time to be in this business. It's never been easier in the 22 years I've been in it than it is right now to go out and do some really, really good kick-butt deals in real estate. I will tell you that the average profit nationwide for my students per deal is about $30,000, and that is climbing rapidly.

Linda: *That's incredible. Ron, what do you say to somebody like myself? I own my home. I have equity in the property. I bought the home for my family. I didn't really buy it from an investment standpoint. You get me excited so I want to go out and become a real estate investor. Say I go out and tell my family, or I go down to a real estate agent and say, "I'm going to be a successful real estate investor," and I get negative feedback from those folks. What do you tell your students when they get that?*

Ron: If you want to be a successful real estate investor why on earth would you go to a real estate agent? How would they know? Real estate agents are in the business of selling properties for commission. Basically they are just self-employed people swapping hours for dollars. Don't get me wrong — I like agents. There's nothing wrong with them. But it's just a job — it just happens to be real estate they're working in. They don't really understand real estate investing.

www.mentorsmagazine.com

Obviously, if you're not careful, they're going to steal your dreams. If they understood real estate investing, they would be doing that instead of selling for a commission. Don't get me wrong, I've got a lot of real estate clients that are licensed real estate agents who are making a killing buying and selling houses while they're simultaneously running their real estate business. There certainly is nothing wrong with that.

But you know, I have a good saying I constantly make sure my students hear from me: "You better be careful to whom you're listening." People who are broke cannot teach you how to get rich. So if you want to learn anything, I don't care what it is, real estate or anything else, the best place to learn is from people who are doing it, not people who are talking about it. The whole country is full of people who would like to give you great advice on a subject they know absolutely nothing about. Now I forgot what the question was!

Linda: *Well, we were just talking about when you get people being negative, stealing your dream of becoming successful in real estate.*

Ron: That's human nature.

Linda: *You work with people who are just starting all the way up to people who are advanced investors. I'm sure there are some people reading this who read the subject of the interview and thought, "I would love to become a real estate investor!" What steps would you recommend someone take if they wanted to work with you and your company to help them? What should their first step be?*

Ron: The first step is to do due diligence and that of course would apply to any business.

I can be found at www.ronlegrand.com. Don't spell it wrong cause all the pirates have got all the misspellings of it. My company is Global Publishing, Inc. At www.globalpublishinginc.com you'll find all about me. In fact, you can just turn on the Internet and type in my name. There are 22,000 websites with my name on them, but only two are our websites: www.ronlegrand.com and www.globalpublishinginc.com.

So the first step anybody ought to do in any kind of business is to follow the fellow who follows his dreams. Go latch onto someone who actually knows what the heck they're talking about. Someone who has been there and done that, is making what you want to make, and who is where you want to be. Unfortunately, there are a lot of people out there teaching real estate who know little more about it than the students. We do a series of seminars and boot camps throughout the country and hands-on training and coaching.

Linda: *Yes, I think that, for whatever reason, in the real estate training industry there are a lot of people out there teaching people how to become successful real*

estate investors but they're not out there doing deals. I think that's one of the great things that makes you unique.

Ron: Since my first seminar back in 1982, I have personally bought and sold over 1,600 single-family houses. I'm still doing it to this very day.

Linda: *Awesome.*

Ron: The latter is most important — still doing it to this very day. Things change from time to time, but we are still on the cutting edge. I'm very lucky. It's fun to be me. It's fun to do what I do. Not only do I help people get rich and save their marriages and actually get their lives back, but I'm also actively doing the real estate business. I stay right on that cutting edge where I know what is going on and I'm fortunate enough to keep up with that. When you're teaching you have to. You don't have any choice if you really care about the quality of your training and the success of your students.

Linda: *What were some of the obstacles that you encountered along the way?*

Ron: Listening to the morons trying to tell me how to run my life and tell me how I don't deserve success. That was one of the first ones. When I came home from one of my very first seminars, my neighbor was one of the guys telling me I was crazy. Six months later, he was suddenly into real estate when I brought home my new BMW. Twenty years later, he's still doing real estate and doing very well at it. It took me a little while to figure out that I really didn't need money or credit to buy real estate. In fact, if I used either one of them I was doing it incorrectly. Once I mastered that one and I was off like a rocket! The biggest mistake I made was not getting the proper training upfront, Linda. So I made a big mess and spent years cleaning up that mess.

Fortunately folks coming into the business don't have to go through that. Of course the men will. There's only two ways to get an education, and us men don't have a choice. We have to do it the hard way! It's testosterone. It's not our fault; we can't help it. If the wheel is round we have to make it rounder.

But for those men who are willing to listen, it doesn't take long to master this business and get big checks coming in quickly. Oh, you'll be a couple of years at it, really mastering the business. Fortunately you don't have to wait to be an expert before you start to make money.

I think one of the biggest things I focus on with people is getting that first check coming in at lightening speed. I realize that as impatient as Americans are, if we don't get some instant gratification we're not going to be around long. There are just too many things pulling at us. So, I work real hard to try to get my students to get their first check within thirty days.

Linda: *Great. Ron, maybe there are some people who would say, "You don't know where I live — it's a tough real estate market here."*

Ron: There's one city in this country where this won't work, Linda.

Linda: *Where is that?*

Ron: It's wherever you live. If you say it won't work where you live, you are absolutely correct. All you can do is move and then it will start working for everybody else.

Linda: *What are some of the factors that make it possible to make money in real estate anywhere in the country?*

Ron: People always have to have a place to live, Linda. Don't ever forget that. We live in a mobile society. When people want out, they want out. I don't care where you are. I've got students in every city, every major city for sure, and almost every minor city in the entire country. I've got people in the high dollar markets like LA, DC and San Francisco. I've got them in the low dollar markets all over the country. In fact, I'd rather be in the high dollar markets because it's a very simple math situation. If you're forced to deal with higher dollar properties, once you learn that it doesn't take money or credit, you'll soon discover the more dollars you wallow in, the more will stick to you. That's Ron's rule. I'll give you an example of one I bought this week. I bought a foreclosure worth $460,000. We paid $310,000 for it, Linda, and I didn't use one dime of my own money.

Linda: *Wow.*

Ron: You know, you only need one of those a week. The house doesn't need one dime's worth of work. It's in excellent condition. So, it doesn't make any difference where you live.

Linda: *Ron, how do you locate properties that are available for a discount?*

Ron: There are all kinds of ways to do that. In fact, in our four-day training events we spend a whole day on that subject because it is critical. There are five steps to this business and the very first one is to locate prospects. Of course, that's the first step to any business. If you don't find people who want to buy your products or services, you're not in business very long, are you?

Linda: *That's right.*

Ron: In our case, we need to find people who have properties for sale. That's really easy to do. They are all over the place, inside and outside the MLS system. Most of our business is with non-listed properties, but there's a whole myriad of things we can do: a direct mail campaign, just running ads or putting up signs, putting up signs on your vehicles, sending out postcards or sending letters to people in pre-foreclosure that have been filed on. That's a matter of public record and an easy list to get. Bankruptcies, divorces. The list is endless.

Linda: *Earlier on in your career it sounded like you had a tremendous amount of risk and now you don't. What are some of the ways you can reduce risk on a real estate deal?*

Ron: Well, I didn't really have a tremendous amount of risk early in my career because I didn't have anything to risk. I didn't have any money or credit, so neither one of those were an issue. Again, the way you eliminate risk is not to write checks to buy properties and not to guarantee debt. Guaranteeing debt will get you in more trouble than any other mistake you can make. I absolutely forbid my students to guarantee debt. We do not go down and suck up to bankers and put in applications and put up down payments to buy real estate. That's the conventional wisdom way, and is not the correct way. It's the way that'll get you in trouble. Of course, we don't make promises we can't keep. So we don't make promises we can't keep, we don't write checks, and we don't guarantee debt. Not much we can do to lose is there?

Linda: *Can you give me an example? What do you mean by guaranteeing debt?*

Ron: When you go down and apply for a loan and you sign on that note, you've just guaranteed that debt with all of your assets. That lender has the ability to come after everything you own until that debt is paid back. And when things don't go the way you expect, that's how you get yourself into a mess. We do not guarantee debt. Now, we take over a lot of debt, but the debt is not in our name. It will not be on our credit report. It is not personally guaranteed debt.

Linda: *So, in the case of the foreclosure property that you recently purchased, you take over the existing note from the former owner?*

Ron: Well, let me give you an example of one here we just completed. That one was an all cash deal. We just bought that one — but it wasn't my cash. That money was borrowed from a private lender. He got a high rate of return secured on the first mortgage on the property, so he's winning and we're winning. We don't have any money in the property. We'll turn around and sell the property within a couple of weeks, take the cash out of it and pay him back. He'll get a nice return and we'll get a nice profit without investing our money. Incidentally, the term "nothing down" is a very misunderstood term. It doesn't necessarily mean the seller doesn't get any money — it's just not any of your money. In this case, the seller got $310,000 cash.

Let me give you another example here. The other day we bought a house for $185,000. The fellow owed $142,000 I think, and the house was in excellent condition — didn't need a thing. He was three payments behind. He called on my

Yellow Pages ad and said, "I just want out of here and I want out of here quick. I don't want any money. I know I'm giving away some equity, but I don't care. If you want it, you've got to come get it quickly."

Of course, those were magic words to us, so my ex-secretary Donna went out and got the deed. Basically she just had the guy transfer ownership of the house right there while she was in the house with him. We took over his loan. We have a signed statement by him that he understands we'll make up the back payments as soon as we put a tenant-buyer in that property.

In that particular case, Linda, our objective is not to go cash out of it and get a cash buyer for it. We're just going to put it on the market and put a lease option on it. We'll have it occupied within the next two weeks, probably with a $10,000 non-refundable option deposit from our tenant-buyer. We'll sell it to them for $185,000 or so. When they get around to going out and getting a loan sometime in the future, at that point we'll cash out. So, we call that "get the deed." We're taking over the loan.

In other words, title is transferred to us on the spot with a simple piece of paper called a deed and the loan will stay in the seller's name until we get it paid off sometime in the future. We will make payments on the property. The money will come from our tenant-buyer to make the underlying payments and the back payments.

So, we have none of our money in the property, we'll make a few thousand dollars upfront very quickly, and we'll make a monthly cash flow from the difference of the rent we're collecting and the payment we're making. I own the property now. I'm depreciating the property so it's reducing my taxes. Then when my tenant buyer gets ready to refinance, we'll get the difference between what they owe us and what we owe. And I bet you didn't understand a word of what I just said, did you? That's a very common deal that I just described to you. I have students doing four, five, six of those a month!

Linda: *And that's what you teach in your programs. You teach people the techniques of how to structure these deals, how you put them together, how you bring in the investor if necessary. That's a lot of what you do, is that true?*

Ron: Quite honestly, a lot of what we do is the kind of deal I just described to you. First of all, there is no investor. We're taking over existing debt. We're not personally liable for it — the seller clearly understands that the loan stays in his or her name. In fact, we'll get them to sign a document that says they do understand that, just to make sure we have a written meeting of the minds. We don't have to put up any money. None was required. We didn't make any promises we couldn't keep. We told him we'd make up the payments when we got the tenant-buyer in the house. We got about $40,000 worth of free equity in a property that's in excellent condition. The value is going to go up every single month. The mortgage amount will go down. We got all the benefits with no risk. Does that make any sense?

Linda: *That makes sense.*

Ron: That's a normal deal, my friend. That's a normal deal and people do it all the time. It's a good example. The profit in that deal will be about $40,000 or more by the time it comes to a conclusion. The best part about it, Linda, is I'm absolutely under no pressure. If I needed to I could write a check to buy the house. It wouldn't hurt me a bit, but that's not the way I do business. I'm under no pressure to pay off that loan in a hurry, no pressure to sell the house quickly. In fact it's not to my advantage to cash out of the house quickly. You see that?

The longer I hold the property, the more profit will be in it. I got it for free. I got several thousand dollars upfront immediately. I'll get more money when they cash out and I'll get a monthly cash flow along the way and a depreciable asset on top of that. Hard to beat. Try that in the stock market! You know what kind of return on an investment that is? Its called infinity. If you don't make an investment, you can't measure the return on it.

Linda: *What does it take to become a successful real estate investor?*

Ron: A little bit of education and a lot of action.

Linda: *How important to you is goal setting?*

Ron: Goal setting is something I think people should do, but I'm not a believer in long-term goals because they get changed. I'm a believer in short-term goals that lead to long-term goals. I think everyone needs to know where they're going or they'll never know when they've arrived. My focus is getting people paid quickly. I know that is a lot more important than goals they create for several years from now. I've just learned that people need to get a check and they need to get it fast. A lot of folks really really need that check. Once they get that check, not only will their commitment level go up but their attention will shift focus from swapping hours for dollars to where it belongs — and that's on creating financial freedom for their entire family. I wish you could see some of these letters I get every week.

Linda: *So it's helping your students get focused on what you can do to make money in your business in the next thirty days?*

Ron: Not only the next thirty days, but consistently thereafter for the rest of your life. I can't tell you how many students we've got out there who are in six-figure incomes their very first year in the business coming out of the job market. Hundreds of them are making over a million dollars a year doing what we're talking about here. I know that's a giant leap for most people, especially when they've had no experience in the real estate business and they've spent their entire life working for a living. We are conditioned to believe that we're not worthy of making that kind of money. That's the way we're brought up. That's what our colleges teach us. Where are you going to learn how to make money if you're not out there in the real world associating with those making real money? They just don't teach this stuff in college.

Linda: *Ron, how did you develop the belief that it was okay to make large sums of money?*

Ron: One check at a time. And they kept getting bigger and bigger and pretty soon I grew to expect them. To this day they're getting bigger and bigger and my expectations are climbing rapidly. My wife says anybody who thinks money won't buy happiness just doesn't know where to shop.

Linda: *Who have been some of your mentors?*

Ron: I can't really tell you that I've had just one mentor. Back in the early days I associated a lot with Mark Harelson, who wrote *How to Wake Up the Financial Genius Inside You*. Mark taught me not only a lot about real estate, but a lot about business. He was important in my life back then. I just went out and grabbed whoever I could get. Anybody who was teaching stuff, I went out and bought it all; anytime I could go to a seminar, I'd find a way to get there. I was a sponge. To this day I'm a sponge. You should see my car; it looks like a tape factory. There's always a tape in the dash or one in the back or in the trunk. It's just kind of a rotating thing. I just rotate until I'm full and then I dump the box and go get some more.

I found that highly successful people are always soaking up information as fast as they can get it, and are always in a learning mode. I think people who quit learning have started the dying process.

Linda: *Ron, one of the things you said earlier was something I've never heard anyone say in this exact way: "Don't make promises you can't keep." What are some of your other philosophies that have served you in business?*

Ron: Probably the biggest and most important lesson I've ever learned in this business that made me a multi-millionaire is a lesson that many people will not incorporate into their lives. It's just not the way they were trained. It is very simple. It is my credo. It is what I live by and it's what I try to instill into my students. It's up on my wall — I'm looking at it right now. I've even got it on a clock. It's these simple words: "The less I do, the more I make."

"The less I do the more I make" means most of what we do every day doesn't mean spit. It doesn't help anybody with anything. It doesn't create any financial independence in our lives. It doesn't do anything to allow wealth to come in.

Most people spend their lives doing everything they can to keep wealth out. All the stuff they do every day has nothing to do with creating wealth. Mostly it's a waste of time. One of the lessons I learned early was if you're going to get filthy stinking rich, you've first got to put yourself in a position to allow it to happen. That's difficult to do when your whole day is spent on minutia, doing all kinds of crap, none of which is going to make you money.

Most people, even those in business for themselves, waste time in the same way every single day. You show me a super wealthy individual and I'll show you someone who doesn't carry a cell phone tagged to their hip, or surgically implanted in their skull, a slave to anyone who wants to call and waste their time anytime they see fit. It's a mindset. It takes a little bit of time to get into that mindset and to ask ourselves all day, every day, "Is this the best use of my time? How am I possibly benefitting myself, my family or anyone else with this crap I'm currently doing?"

Linda: *So is part of it changing the activities, changing daily actions to allow that wealth to come in?*

Ron: Yes, part of it is to take time to focus on the important things — not only the financial things, but also the important things. I mean, people lose sight of why they're in business sometimes. They get sucked into the business. A business is supposed to support you, the owner. It's not to support employees, it's not to provide jobs — it's to support a living for the owner. When we own our businesses, sometimes we forget that and our life is in supporting-the-business mode. All of our hours and all the money that we get are thrown back into the business. That's not the way to get wealthy. That's the way to swap hours for dollars and basically just exchange one employed boss for a self-employed boss. You don't accomplish anything like that.

Some people say, "I want to get in business for myself so I only have to work half a day." You've just got to decide which twelve hours it is, Linda. Because its easy to be busy. A rat in a cage running around in a circle can be busy, but they don't accomplish anything. I find that to be the exact truth for most people, especially the self-employed people. It's a hard thing to stop all the junk you've been doing all your life — wasting time — and start focusing on doing the important stuff. For example, I can't imagine why anybody would want to mow their own lawn or repair their own houses. People sometimes tell me, "Well, it's my therapy." I tell them if you want to repair your own house, you need therapy.

Linda: *Ron, what are some of those activities, then? What you're saying is the most important key to success is making sure you're taking actions on things that are making a difference for you and creating wealth. What would you suggest some of those activities be?*

Ron: There are five steps to success in this or any other business. In fact, I challenge the readers to write these down and apply them to the business they may be in — or may be thinking about — because there is not a business on the planet that these five steps don't apply to. Number one is to locate prospects. I don't care what business, product, service or whatever, you better find somebody who wants that product or service or you're not going to be around long. In our business that's people with houses for sale. We first have to buy them and then we'll do the same five steps in selling them. We have to locate prospects who want to buy them from us.

The second step is to pre-screen those prospects. There's a huge difference between suspects and prospects, Linda. Suspects are people who want to sell their house. Prospects are people who need to sell it. Suspects will get you out of the business very quickly, because they'll convince you there is nobody out there who's motivated and really needs to sell. Suspects want to pre-screen you and make you justify your existence on this planet and why they should allow you the opportunity and the privilege of buying their property. Prospects will do whatever you want them to do because you're giving them the opportunity of getting out of that property. You're actually giving them stress relief, giving them their life back and usually giving them debt relief. If you don't quickly recognize the difference between suspects and prospects, you won't be around long. Suspects will steal your dreams. Prospects will make you filthy stinking rich. That's true in any business, Linda, in any business. Most people spend too much time dealing with people who really don't want to deal with them. You can't make an unmotivated seller motivated. You have to find the people who are motivated and whack the rest at lightening speed.

The third step is to construct and present offers. I don't care what business you're in. If you want someone to buy your products and services, you have to give them the opportunity to do that and tell them why they should. In our business, fortunately there's real good news: there are only three different kinds of offers we have to make on properties to produce 90% of our revenue. The other 10% are things we can do, but rarely get a chance to do.

There are only two or three ways we need to learn to buy properties to get the checks coming in and keep them coming in. I suggest to my students that we do that. Let's get the easy money coming in first. Then, we expand our horizons and get really good at this business after we get our cash flow needs of today taken care of. Constructing and presenting offers is the key that unlocks the vault.

The fourth step is follow up. In this case that means those people who have passed the pre-screening tests are worthy of our following up later because we know they need to sell. They're just not ready right now. Here is what I know: all sellers' minds will change with time and circumstance. When the time is right and the circumstance is right, you're there and they know you're there.

You may very well be the one that buys that property when your competition has long since given up. In fact, most businesses are one-hit-wonders. They get a "no" once and they're out of here.

Linda, did you know that 82% of all buying decisions are made between the second and the seventh contact with a prospect? Someone who gives up that quickly has decided they'll take an 82% pay cut.

"Follow up" also means taking care of the details once you have arrived at an agreement with the seller who is selling you the home. The first thing we have to do when we get a deed or contract is to have the title checked. That's a phone call, but it's a very important phone call. We have to make sure there are no problems that will keep us from selling the property, which is step five: sell quickly.

We've got to get in, we've got to get out and we've got to get the cash because nothing happens until something is sold. It's that cash that creates the revenue we need to enjoy this business. Without that cash we're not going to like this business. When I started, I was told to go out and buy a bunch of properties, put tenants in them and pretty soon you'll wake up rich. True or false, what do you think?

Linda: *False.*

Ron: Oh no, it's true. Go buy properties, put a bunch of tenants in them, and you will wake up rich, someday.

Linda: *Right.*

Ron: They forgot to tell me what happens between now and someday. You know, I tell my students the first thing you ought to focus on is taking care of today's cash flow needs before you worry about getting rich. The last thing, the very last thing that a brand new real estate entrepreneur needs is a tenant. The first thing they need is a check.

Now I don't have anything against tenants. I think that the true wealth in real estate or any other business is from the equity, but in order to get to the equity tomorrow we need cash flow today. So we've got to focus on creating some dollars out of these things — spendable cash. When we get that fixed, we can start looking at real estate as a wealth-builder by keeping some of the properties and not selling everything we get our hands on.

Linda: *Ron, would you like to talk about one or two of your programs that you think would be a good step for the listeners?*

Ron: If they go to www.ronlegrand.com they'll get an idea of what we're all about. We have live training; we have home study courses and coaching. We have mentoring. I mean, we have every base covered in the real estate business. Anybody who's serious and wants to get in it, we're there for them.

Global Publishing Inc. is actually run by my daughter. In fact, the whole company is run by women, so that ought to tell you something. It's done right, you know? When you get involved with us, you're actually joining a family that is creating a lifetime relationship — not only with us, but with all the students you run across when we get you in the live events out there.

It's a beautiful thing when you get trained and you actually create relationships that go on for the rest of your life. Can't tell you how many of our students have created cross-country relationships and are just doing some really cool things because of the people they meet in these live events. What a great place to meet people that you ought to be associated with; people with the same upwardly-mobile objectives and people with real estate on their mind. It's amazing how small this country really is, Linda, when you put people from all over it in one room.

Linda: *Thank you Ron for an incredibly informative and inspiring interview! Ladies and gentlemen, I strongly encourage you to contact Ron and attend his seminars. It will change your life! Check out some of the testimonials included in this printing.*

Dear Ron,

Nine months ago I went to your MMBC. When I returned home, my employer fired me because they said I was away too long, and I didn't have the time to cover my trip. I knew it was because they were having financial difficulties, and they wanted to thin out the staff. That made up my mind right there that I didn't want anyone ever controlling my time again, telling me when I can travel or how long I can be gone or firing me because they have money problems. If they had not let me go I would probably still be there day in and day out, wishing I could start investing. They did me a BIG favor!

Since I've been investing with your system over the past six months (since I've been serious), I have closed five deals. One was an immediate flip where I made $12,000. Then I bought two fixer uppers and I've done two short sales. This year I have already made $46,000 in cash and I have $75,000 waiting for me in equity. That is way more than my previous salary of $24,000. Gee, how did I live on that?

Tim & Arlene Thomas
Albuquerque, New Mexico

Dear Ron,

Just a couple of weeks ago I received some literature from you. I opened it up and was floored to see my letter on the very first page. To say the least, I am speechless and humbled to think that just over a year ago I spent three hours every morning (3am – 6am) driving my paper route, to make ends meet, listening to the Red, Blue, & Green "mods" and hearing the awesome testimonials of other success stories. To think back at how I longed for that, and to see now that I *am* that, it is unbelievable! I had no doubt from the first time I began to study your systems that I would end up where I am today!

At the beginning of March, during spring break, I had taken my family on a fun-filled shopping spree to the Dallas area. (We had never been able to do anything like this before.) It happened just like you said; we were able to go where we wanted, do what we wanted, stay as long as we wanted, and buy what we wanted! We stayed in an exclusive hotel, ordered room service, and really lived it up! To add icing to the cake, the last morning we were there, I received a call from my title company letting me know they were closing one of my deals in which I would be getting a check for a little over $15,000. The property had been deeded to me only a few weeks prior. Needless to say we ordered lunch off of the left side of the menu that day!

Roger Ketchum
Gladewater, Texas

Find out more about **Ron LeGrand** *and Global Publishing Inc. at ronlegrand.com, globalpublishinginc.com, www.goffn.com, or call 1-800-567-6128*

Move Forward with Boldness
on Your Quest
and Might Forces
Will Come to Your Aid

Mentors Magazine Motto

INVEST IN
YOUR SUCCESS ...

Tapes, Books, Boot Camps, Seminars,

Newsletters, and Coaching from our

Walking with the Wise Real Estate

contributors are available at:

www.mentorsmagazine.com